THE GREAT COUNCIL TAX RECOVERY SCAM
APPROVED BY THE MAGISTRATES & JUDGES
HOW TO CHALLENGE THEIR COSTS

PAUL PATTESON

Copyright © 2020 Paul Patterson

All rights reserved.

ISBN: 9798678964274

CONTENTS

Chapter		
	Introduction	Pg 5
1	The Summons	Pg 7
2	How To Request A Copy Of The Council's Breakdown Of Costs	Pg 12
3	Application To State A Case	Pg 38
4	Refusal To State A Case	Pg 41
5	Application For Judicial Review	Pg 46
6	Hull City Council	Pg 54
7	Nottingham Council	Pg 61
8	Lambeth Council	Pg 65
9	Barnet Borough Council	Pg 73
10	Ashford Borough Council	Pg 81
	Conclustion	Pg 85

A LITTLE EXTRA

Enforcement Agents Entered The Wrong Property For The wrong Person	Pg 88
Attachment Of Earnings	Pg 130
Amount Cornwall Council Were Overchaged For Summonses By The Ministry Of Justice	Pg 131
A Template Legal Notice Challenging Rochdale Borough Councils summons costs	Pg 135

INTRODUCTION

Those of you who have ever fallen in arrears with council tax will be well aware of the councils' procedure.

Reminder notice
Firstly you will receive a reminder notice, which will state you need to bring your account up to date within 7 days. If payment is not received as requested on the reminder notice, recovery action may continue and a summons issued.

If you make payment of the sum requested on the reminder notice, no further action is taken as long as you continue to make payment of your remaining monthly instalments on time.

Final notice
The council will only issue two reminder notices to you during one financial year.

If you are late paying for a third time in a year, you will be issued with a final notice, which will cancel your monthly instalments.

Your instalment plan will only be reinstated if you bring your instalments up to date and set up a direct debit to ensure future payments are made on time.

If payment is not received as requested on the final notice, recovery action will continue and a summons issued.

So, you can find yourself being summonsed to the magistrates' court for owing as little as one month of arrears.

What people are not aware of is that councils all over the country are acting unlawful, they are highly inflating their costs in summonsing people to court. Councils can only charge for reasonable costs 'incurred.'

Because of the covid-19 restrictions it looks like there will be no summonses sent out in 2020 for the tax year 2020-2021. This is because councils summons people in bulk listings of 1,000 –2,000 people all invited to turn up to court on the same day, at the same time. (*** Page 85) & (Page 135)** This is why the council states on their summonses that you do not need to attend, the council and magistrates don't want you to attend. That way the council gets their bulk liability order listing approved in minutes.

Everyone who receives a council tax summons needs to attend their hearing, in doing so this will create chaos and panic for councils and magistrates. This book will show you how to challenge the councils on their highly inflated costs.

This book will show the evidence that magistrates and judges are approving the council's highly inflated costs, allowing councils to act unlawfully and fraudulently.

CHAPTER 1

THE SUMMONS

The abolition of the old poll tax was announced on 21 March 1991.

As the amount of the poll tax began to rise and the inefficiency of local councils in their collection of the tax became apparent, large numbers of people refused to pay. Local councils tried to respond with enforcement measures, but they were largely ineffective given the large numbers of non-payers.

It wasn't the Poll Tax riots of 31 March 1990 – when between 70,000 and 200,000 people demonstrated around Trafalgar Square that brought the poll tax down. It was the large numbers of former ratepayers refusing to pay, up to 30% in some areas.

At the time these huge numbers of non-payers had to be individually summonsed to court, this is what brought down the poll tax, not the riots. Because non-payers were being summonsed individually, it was taking 18 months or more to summons the non-payers individually.

So the regulations were changed in The Council Tax (Administration and Enforcement) Regulations 1992. The new regulations allowed councils to apply to the magistrates' court with a bulk listing of all the non-payers that they wished to have summonsed to the court. On the day of the hearing the council would present this list to the magistrates who would then grant liability orders against every name on the bulk listing. Once granted, the local authority passes the liability orders to the court to be signed by the Justices Clerk. This is simply a list of all names heard in court with the orders noted against them.

A liability order is not a 'court order' it is simply a statement that a debt is owed.

Liability orders: further provision
35. – (3)…'it is not to be treated as a sum adjudged to be paid by order of the court'…
https://www.legislation.gov.uk/uksi/1992/613/regulation/35/made

Everyone who is summonsed for non-payment of council tax has a lawful right to challenge the councils' costs which the councils claim they have incurred to bring non-payers to court.

So, as soon as a non-payers receives a council summons for non-payment, they must immediately contact the council and magistrates court, and request a copy of the council's breakdown of their cost for council tax summonses which the magistrates have approved. It is usual for the magistrates to approve these costs at the beginning of each tax year, then these costs are claimed at each council tax hearing throughout the year.

The case of Nicolson, R (on the application of) v Tottenham Magistrates & Anor [2015] EWHC 1252 (Admin) dated back to 2 August 2013 when Reverend Paul Nicolson was ordered to pay £125 costs to Haringey Council for obtaining a liability order. The vicar had refused to pay his council tax in protest at changes to council tax benefits.

Rev Nicolson asked the magistrates how the £125 sum had been arrived at. (In 2011 the council had requested an increase in costs from £95 to £125)

On 20 December 2013 Tottenham Magistrates refused to state a case in respect of the order of costs.

Under Regulation 34(7) of the Council Tax (Administration and Enforcement) Regulations 1992 (SI 1992 No.613) a court, when granting a liability order, shall make an order reflecting the aggregate of the outstanding council tax and "a sum of an amount equal to the costs reasonably incurred by the applicant in obtaining the order."

In England there is no legislative cap on those costs; in Wales there is a proviso that the costs "including those of instituting the application under paragraph (2), are not to exceed the prescribed amount of £70."

Rev Nicolson's challenge to the legality of the costs order focused on the absence of information that he said was necessary for the Magistrates to address their minds to the question whether the essential causal connection between the costs claimed and the obtaining of the order had been established by the council.

This was allied with a complaint that the Magistrates appeared "to have confused the reasonableness of the amount of the costs with the question whether that sum was reasonably incurred", Mrs Justice Andrews said. (judge's emphasis)

The judge concluded that Rev Nicolson was entitled to have the information he requested in order that he could form a view as to whether the proposed order was within the powers of the Magistrates under Regulation 34(7) and make submissions on it.

Counsel for Haringey had submitted that the Magistrates had sufficient material to enable them to make the decision, but Mrs Justice Andrews said it was "patent that they did not".

She added: "In fact, they had no material which would have justified them in reaching the conclusion that the costs that were claimed were incurred in connection with the issue of the summons or obtaining the liability order.

"All they had was the say-so of a Council representative, who was unable to give any better explanation when he was challenged than (at most) the vague statements recorded in the Magistrates' reasons for refusal to state a case." (Judge's emphasis)

Mrs Justice Andrews said she also considered that the decision was unlawful because the claimant had not been provided, on request, with the information that would have enabled him to make properly informed submissions on whether the costs claimed were reasonably incurred in obtaining the liability order.

"It is immaterial that he made no request from the council for disclosure before the hearing," she added. "There was no requirement on him to do so. It was perfectly proper for the claimant to expect that the Magistrates would be able to provide him with information as to what costs were comprised in the £125 and how that figure was calculated, since they needed to know that information in order to discharge their legal duties."

Mrs Justice Andrews was told at the hearing that the order for costs against Rev Nicolson had already been withdrawn. Had that not been the case, she said, she would have quashed it.

In summary, the judge declared the order to be unlawful because:

The Magistrates did not have sufficient relevant information before them to reach a proper judicial determination of whether the costs claimed represented costs reasonably incurred by the council in obtaining the liability order;

The Magistrates erred in law by failing to make further inquiries into how the £125 was computed and what elements it comprised; and
the claimant was denied a fair opportunity to challenge the lawfulness of the order before it was made, by reason of the failure to answer his requests for the provision of information as to how the sum of £125 was arrived at.

Mrs Justice Andrews ordered Haringey to play the claimant's pro bono costs, and the fees, costs and expenses that he incurred earlier in the case, when he was acting in person.

Helen Mountfield QC and Eloise Le Santo of Matrix Chambers appeared for the vicar in the High Court, instructed by the Bar Pro Bono Unit.

Rev Nicolson said: "I made the challenge because I know £125 costs is a very big penalty on top of the inevitable council tax arrears, rent arrears and sanctions for the 1000s of benefit claimants in work and unemployment who have been charged the council tax by Haringey Council since April 2013."

He added that he had called on Grant Thornton, external auditors to Haringey, to produce a report in the public interest about the £125 level of costs. These were increased from £95 in 2011.

A Haringey Council spokesperson said: "We accept the court's decision to quash the costs order in this case as magistrates did not have the relevant information before them.

"We welcome that the judge accepted our broad approach to calculating costs to cover legal proceedings. We will now consider this ruling in greater detail."

It is important to note paragraph 46 of Mrs Justice Andrews approved judgement: -
"In principal, therefore, provided that the right types of costs and expenses are taken into account, and provided that due consideration is given to the dangers of double counting, or of artificial inflation of costs, it may be a legitimate approach for local authorities to calculate and

aggregate the relevant costs it has incurred in the previous year, and divide that up by the previous (or anticipated) number of summonses over twelve months so as to provide an average figure which could be levied across the board in "standard" cases, but could be amplified in circumstances where there was justification for incurring additional legal and/or administrative costs. If that approach is adopted, however it is essential that the magistrates and their clerks are equipped with sufficient readily available information to enable the magistrates to check for themselves without too much difficulty, and relatively swiftly, that a legitimate approach has been taken, and to furnish a respondent with that information on request."

CHAPTER 2

HOW TO REQUEST A COPY OF THE COUNCIL'S BREAKDOWN OF COSTS.

The best way to make these requests is by way of a Freedom of Information request, but to do this you would need to make the request long before you receive a summons as this can take some weeks. https://www.whatdotheyknow.com/

Example:
https://www.whatdotheyknow.com/request/a_breakdown_of_staffing_costs_an#incoming-1395353

Dear Cornwall Council,

Will you please send me copies of the breakdown of staffing costs and calculation approved by the magistrates for council tax summonses for:
2010-2011
2012-2013
2013-2014
2014-2015
2015-2016
2016-2017
2017-2018
2019-2020

Yours faithfully,

Paul Patterson.

The replies you will receive from these requests will enable you to challenge the council's costs. You will also uncover the council's highly inflated costs, which are unlawful, fraudulent and deceitful.

The following is the reply I received for my above request:

Reference Number: FOI 101004533959

Response provided under: Freedom of Information Act 2000

Request:
Please provide me with the following information under the Freedom of Information Act 2000.

Will you please send me copies of the breakdown of staffing costs and calculation approved by the magistrates for council tax summonses for:

2010-2011
2012-2013
2013-2014
2014-2015
2015-2016
2016-2017
2017-2018
2019-2020

Response:

We do not hold a breakdown of staffing costs and calculation approved by the magistrates for council tax summonses prior to 2015.

The breakdown of staffing costs and calculation approved by the magistrates for council tax summonses for the period 2015 to October 2018:

Summons	Description	Cost

	Production, printing, packing & posting	£2.23
	Admin	£55.46
Liability Order	**Description**	**Cost**
	Production, printing, packing & posting	£2.23
	Admin	£18.60
Court Fee		£3.00
	Total	**£81.52**

Please see the attached PDF for the breakdown of staffing costs and calculation approved by the magistrates for council tax summonses for the period November 2018 to date.

Information provided by: Customer Access and Digital Services (Revenues)

From the information I received from a number of Freedom of Information Request it allowed me to challenge Cornwall Council on their highly inflated costs.

My hearing was for the 29th May 2019 I attended the court early and handed my legal notice to the clerk to the justices to hand to the three magistrates. The three magistrates entered the courtroom, then to my surprise the chair of the magistrates stated that she has never seen a well presented case as this, and she would have to adjourn the hearing for four weeks to give the council time to respond.

So the hearing was adjourned until 27th June 2019 where on my attendance I was surprised that the magistrates had been removed from the case and replaced with a district judge.

Paul Patterson

LEGAL NOTICE
22nd June 2019

FAO

Bodmin Magistrates

Alessandro Roveri Clerk to the Justices

Bodmin Legal Team

Dear Bodmin Court,

I was originally invited via a Council summons received from Cornwall Council inviting me to appear before the magistrates sitting at Bodmin Magistrates Court on 18th April 2019. I sent the court and Cornwall Council for that hearing my legal notice dated 10th April 2019.

On my request the hearing was adjourned until 29th May 2019.

One of the requests in my legal notice dated 10th April 2019 was for the court to:-

'Disclose Cornwall Council's break down of costs,' as adding unreasonable costs to the claim is unlawful.

On receiving from the court the Council's breakdown of costs, **[Exhibit A]** I soon **realised that these costs are highly inflated.**

This legal notice is for the new hearing date 27th June 2019.

INDEX

PAGE 2………………..	INDEX	
PAGE 3………………..	SKELETON ARGUMENT	
PAGE 4………………..	STATEMENT OF GROUNDS	
PAGE 11………………..	EXHIBIT A	The councils costs and calculations 2018-19
PAGE 12………………..	EXHIBIT B	Freedom of information response.
PAGE 13………………..	EXHIBIT C	Customer Access and Digital Services Structure Chart.
PAGE 14………………..	EXHIBIT D	The salaries of all the named job titles on the customer services flow chart.
PAGE 16………………..	EXHIBIT E	Breakdown of payments made on Credit Card from Cornwall Council to HMCTS 2018-19
PAGE 17 ………………..	EXHIBIT F	The councils calculation of costs 2016-17 approved by magistrates.
PAGE 18………………….	EXHIBIT G	Email confirming Raul DeMenezes considered the complaint.
PAGE 21………………….	EXHIBIT H	Email confirming the person whose signature appears on the summons 'MUST' have personally considered the complaint.

PAGE 23............................**EXHIBIT I** Summons with signature of Clerk to the Justices Alessandro Roveri.

SKELETON ARGUMENT

1. **That the Court allowed unlawful and unjustified costs added to the applications.**

2. **The court has never carried out any calculations of the Council's costs to valuate if they are reasonable incurred costs. They have only taken the Court officer's word.**

3. **I suspect that the costs are being used as a form of penalty or deterrent, or as a means of covering the Council's general administrative costs of collecting council tax, rather than reflecting any actual or fair appraisal of the actual costs incurred by them in enforcing the obligation to pay.**

4. **The magistrates have been approving costs for, production, printing, packaging and posting of liability orders, which are not printed.**

5. **I challenge the validity of the summons.**

I also bring the following to the courts attention:

I claim the Council has breached High Court Case ruling of: CO/976/2014

Rev Paul Nicholson v Tottenham Magistrates, because adding unreasonable

costs to the claim was unlawful.

The Council Tax (Administration and Enforcement) Regulations 1992
34(7) An order made pursuant to paragraph (6) shall be made in respect of an amount equal to the aggregate of—

(a) the sum payable, and
(b) a sum of an amount equal to the costs reasonably incurred by the applicant in obtaining the order.

STATEMENT OF GROUNDS

1.

'The Court Officer' which there is two of, Adrian Walters and Lynda Ryan, which is very confusing as neither work for the court.

Exhibit A states:

Court Officer **has an allocated time of 12 minutes to process each summons @ cost of £3.72 each.**

The two Court Officers are contracted to work 37 hours a week, 1,250 hours per year.

These two Court Officers can only process between them 12,500 summonses per year working full-time at 5 summonses each per hour. There would need to be 4 full-time Officers.

1250 hours = 75,000 mins
12mins = 6,250 summonses

If they were to state but no, we process 10 each per hour, well this would mean their cost per summons would have to be reduced to £1.86 per summons to be reasonable. Clearly highly inflated costs.

Revenues and Assessments Manager.

Can only process 15,000 per year, would need to be 2 of these officers full-time

1250 hours = 75,000 mins
5mins = 15,000 summonses

Revenues Team Leader.

Can only process 7,500 summonses per year, would need 8 full-time managers to process summonses & liability orders.

**1250 hours = 75,000 mins
10mins = 7,500 summonses
10mins = 7,500 liability orders.**

Senior Revenues Officer.

**Can only process 4,687 summons per year would need 5 full-time Officers.
16mins = 4,687 summonses (8 mins left over)**

10mins = 7,500 liability orders would need 3 full-time Officer.

Exhibit B **Clearly states there is no job tittle of a Senior Revenues Officer working for Cornwall Council.**

Recovery Officer.

**Full-time Officer.
1250 hours = 75,000 mins
1.35hrs = 95mins = 789 summonses (45 mins left over) would need 31 Officers working full-time.**

43mins = 1,744 liability orders. Would need 11 Officers working full-time.

(8mins left over)

Exhibit B **Clearly states the Recovery Officers don't work in collection of council tax, but work in housing benefits even so, there are only 6 of those Officers.**

Exhibit B **states:**

"We do not employ staff for the sole purpose of Council Tax recovery work.

Multi skilled officers within the Revenues and Assessment team are involved in the daily administration of recovery work, in addition to processing other Revenues & Assessment work.

The Recovery Officers shown in the Organisational Chart refer to Housing Benefit Overpayment Recovery Officers."

2.

It is clear that these Cornwall Council's costs have been highly inflated, and the magistrates have never calculated these costs. They have only took the Court Officers word.

There would need to be 64 Officers working full-time according to the Councils cost sheet.

According to the statement in Exhibit B and the Organisational Chart Exhibit C at most there are 68 Officers, neither working full-time on summonses and liability orders but Multi skilled, working in other Revenues & Assessment work.

<u>3.</u>

An extract from:

<u>Rev Paul Nicholson v Tottenham Magistrates, because adding unreasonable costs to the claim was unlawful.</u>

23. The Claimant pointed out the serious consequences that orders of this type can have on some of the poorest people in society, and the anxiety which the making and consequences of such orders can cause. He made this observation (with which I agree): Mrs Justice Andrews.

"The making of such an order is not, therefore, a matter of rubber-stamping, but one in respect of which it is vital that the due process of law is observed."

<u>The legal obligations of the Magistrates</u>

33. The proceedings before the Magistrates were civil in nature, but the Civil Procedure Rules do not apply to them. Thus there is no provision for the assessment of costs, as there would be in normal civil litigation. By contrast with the Civil Procedure Rules, there are no provisions in the Regulations requiring the costs to be reasonable or proportionate, nor is there any requirement that any doubt be resolved in favour of the paying party. The Magistrates were bound to decide the matter of costs in accordance with the Regulations.

34. As a matter of straightforward construction of Regulation 34(7) that means that the Magistrates must be satisfied:
i)   that the local authority has actually incurred those costs;
ii)   that the costs in question were incurred in obtaining the liability order; and

iii)   that it was reasonable for the local authority to incur them.

35. It is clear that there must be a sufficient link between the costs in question and the process of obtaining the liability order. It would obviously be impermissible (for example) to include in the costs claimed any element referable to the costs of executing the order after it was obtained, or to the overall administration of council tax in the area concerned.
36 Since the question whether the costs claimed in this case were "reasonably incurred in obtaining the liability order" is not a matter I have to decide and I have not heard argument on it, it seems to me that I should be circumspect in any observations that I make which could have a bearing on that issue should it arise on a future occasion. On the other hand, there are no authorities that specifically address these Regulations, and this is an opportunity for the Court to afford some general guidance as to their interpretation and scope.

37. I doubt whether any assistance in this regard can be derived from authorities in relation to the CPR or the pre-CPR costs regimes, as the Regulations do not refer to "costs of the proceedings". There is some limited assistance to be derived from the Regulations themselves as to what kinds of costs are included. Regulation 34(5) sets out the circumstances in which the application for a liability order shall not be proceeded with. The respondent must pay or tender to the local authority any unpaid council tax plus "a sum of an amount equal to the costs reasonably incurred by the authority in connection with the application up to the time of payment or tender."

38. Ms Henderson submitted, and Ms Mountfield agreed, that if such costs were recoverable at the stage in between issue of the summons and hearing for the liability order, they must necessarily be subsumed in the expression "costs reasonably incurred in obtaining the order" in Regulation 34(7). Otherwise there would be no incentive to the respondent to pay the council tax before the hearing. I agree that as a matter of necessary implication, and for the policy reason referred to by counsel, costs incurred in obtaining the order must encompass costs incurred in connection with the application for a summons. Plainly the costs would encompass, but are not confined to, the fee for issuing the summons: the expression "in connection with the application" is wider than "the costs of making the application". However, there still has to be a sufficient link between the incurring of those costs and the application for a summons.

39. Ms Henderson submitted that the expression "costs" is not necessarily confined to legal costs and that in other contexts it has been held to encompass time spent in investigations and elements of administrative costs. She referred to R v Tottenham Justices ex parte Joshi [1982] 1 WLR 631 in which the Divisional Court decided that the statutory discretion to award costs in criminal proceedings was wide enough to cover the time of an investigating officer paid out of public funds whose job it was to investigate alleged offences, and time spent by clerical staff. However, as Ms Henderson frankly admitted, it is difficult to draw any analogy between council tax and the scope of costs awarded to prosecuting authorities in criminal cases, because in the latter scenario there is a discretion to award costs. Moreover, as in cases falling under the CPR, it is possible to have an assessment of the reasonableness and proportionality of the costs; and the nature of the criminal investigations is very different.

40. Ms Henderson pointed out that before it makes its application, the local authority has to be satisfied that it is requesting the issue of a summons for the right amount of tax against the right respondent, and that may take up staff time, which is a cost to it. She submitted that it was at least arguable that such administrative or investigatory costs fell within the expression "in connection with the making of the application." She also submitted that the costs of deciding whether or not to exercise the discretion to enforce could properly be included.

41. Ms Mountfield accepted that the expression "in connection with" might extend to some administrative expenses and overheads provided they were properly referable to taking enforcement steps against the respondent. She submitted that, for example, it was arguable that the expression might be interpreted as extending to the administrative costs and expenses of issuing

and serving final notices in those cases in which the local authority then goes on to seek a summons, because they are a compulsory step without which the application for a summons against that respondent cannot be made. On the other hand, it would be difficult (if not impossible) to establish the necessary connection between the enforcement process and costs incurred by a local authority in the normal course of events, such as the costs of sending out reminder notices to taxpayers.

42. It seems to me that in principle the intention in the Regulations is to enable the local authority to recover the actual cost to it of utilising the enforcement process under Regulation 34, which is bound to include some administrative costs, as well as any legal fees and out of pocket expenses, always subject to the overarching proviso that the costs in question were reasonably incurred. However, bearing in mind the court's inability to carry out any independent assessment of the reasonableness of the amount of those costs, the Regulations should be construed in such a way as to ensure that the costs recovered are only those which are genuinely attributable to the enforcement process.

43. Apart from the costs of the final notice, which can arguably be justified on the specific basis adverted to by Ms Mountfield, (though only in those cases where a summons is issued) it seems to me, both as a matter of language and purposive interpretation, that it would be difficult to justify including any other costs incurred prior to the decision being taken to enforce (which is a matter of discretion under Regulation 34(1)). In order for costs to be incurred in connection with the making of the application, a decision to make such an application must have been taken. It is only then that the process of enforcement gets underway. Indeed Regulation 34(5), which includes that phrase, is specifically addressing the scenario where a summons has been issued, and thus the decision to enforce has been taken.

I suspect that the costs are being used as a means of covering the Council's general administrative costs of collecting council tax, rather than reflecting any actual or fair appraisal of the actual costs incurred by them in enforcing the obligation to pay.

When adding up the salaries of staff in EXHIBIT D **with the job tittles in** EXHIBIT B **they pretty much add up to the staffing costs in** EXHIBIT A

4.

The magistrates have been approving costs for, production, printing, packaging and posting of liability orders, which are not printed.
Refer to EXHIBIT E & F

5.
A court legal adviser has stated, 'The summons must be authorised by a Justice of the Peace or by the Clerk to the Justices, and the person whose signature appears on the summons must have personally considered the complaint. A Justice's Clerk is empowered to consider a complaint and issue a summons, in the manner of a Justice of the Peace, by the Justice's Clerks Rules. The task of signing a summons can be performed by the use of a facsimile signature, or a rubber-stamped signature, of the Justice of the Peace or the Justice's Clerk signature. The reference to a Justices' Clerk
includes a Legal Adviser.'

It is excepted that a legal adviser can be delegated to consider a complaint, and reference to a Justices' Clerk includes a Legal Adviser. But, the Legal Adviser if considering the complaint should also have his/her signature on the summons for the complaint he/her considered.

Because the wrong signature is on the summon, I challenge the validity of the summons.

EXHIBIT G confirms Raul DeMenezes was the legal adviser who considered the complaint.

EXHIBIT H Email confirming that the person whose signature appears on the summons must have personally considered the complaint.

EXHIBIT I Summons with signature of Clerk to the Justices Alessandro Roveri.

All the above clearly shows the council have highly inflated their costs.

Yours faithfully,
Paul Patterson.

EXHIBIT A

Summary | Calcs | Sheet3

Cornwall Council

Business Rates and Council Tax Summons and Liability Orders Charges 2018/19

Staff costs include all overheads applicable as calculated in the rate card for the authority.
The rate card is used for internal and external charging of staff time.

	Summons Volume	Liability Order Volume
Business Rates	1,847	1,147
Council Tax	23,046	19,529

Staff Costs

Position Title	Time allocated Summons (Hours)	Time allocated Liability Orders (Hours)	Time Cost per Summons (£)	Time Cost per Liability Order (£)
Revenues and Assessments Manager.	0.05	0.00	£2.60	£0.00
Revenues Team Leader.	0.10	0.10	£3.60	£3.60
Senior Revenues Officer.	0.16	0.10	£4.96	£3.10
Court Officer.	0.12	0.00	£3.72	£0.00
Recovery Officer.	1.35	0.43	£41.85	£13.33
Costs per Summons / Liability Order			**£56.73**	**£20.03**

Staff cost total			£1,412,180	£414,140
Printing, packing, posting of 14 day letter (£0.41 per summons)			£10,206	£0
Court Cost 50p per Summons			£12,446	£0
Total Cost per summons / liability order			**£57.64**	**£20.03**

Dedicated Court Officers Capacity

	Contracted hours each per week	Chargeable hours each per year	Summons	Liability Orders	Capacity for Summons and Liability Orders
Court Officer x 2	37	1,250	0.1	inclusive	25,000

Hourly rate Inclusive Costs

These are the costs applicable for the provision of any Cornwall Council employee.

Cost Type	Average Percentage of hourly rate attributable to each cost type
Salary	60.6%
National Insurance	6.4%
Superannuation	10.6%
Travel	1.1%
Training	1.1%
Office provisions	0.4%
Administrative overhead	6.3%
Management Overhead	12.9%
Other Direct Costs e.g professional subs	0.6%

EXHIBIT B

Reference Number: FOI 101004430152

Response provided under: Freedom of Information Act 2000

Request:
Please provide me with the following information under the Freedom of Information Act 2000.

Could I now request that you send me the following information please:

How many persons were employed by Cornwall Council to each of the following job descriptions full time/part time and their contracted hours each week for 2018/19

1. REVENUES AND ASSESSMENTS MANAGER

2. REVENUES TEAM LEADER

3. SENIOR REVENUES OFFICER

4. COURT OFFICER

5. RECOVERY OFFICER

Response:

Please see the Customer Access and Digital Services Structure Chart attached, which provides the above requested information.

A full time officer is employed to work 37 hours per week.

You will note that within the chart that we do not list Senior Revenues Officers, please refer to Revenues Officers, and Revenues and Assessment Assistants.

We do not employ staff for the sole purpose of Council Tax recovery work. Multi skilled officers within the Revenues and Assessment team are involved in the daily administration of recovery work, in addition to processing other Revenues & Assessment work.
The Recovery Officers shown in the Organisational Chart refer to Housing Benefit Overpayment Recovery Officers.

Information provided by: Customer Access and Digital Services (Revenues)

EXHIBIT C

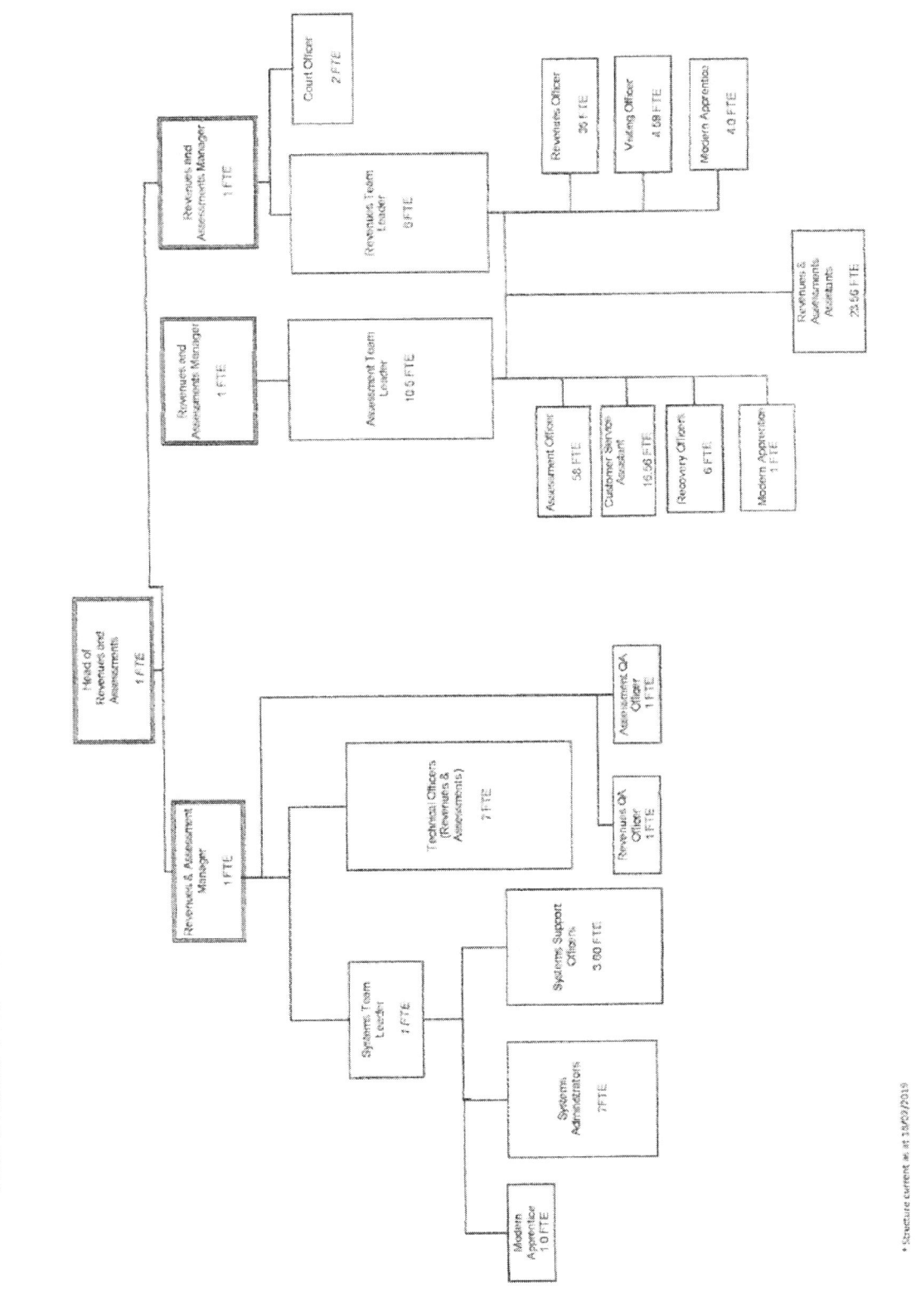

Revenues and Assessments

- Head of Revenues and Assessments — 1 FTE
  - Revenues and Assessments Manager — 1 FTE
    - Court Officer — 2 FTE
    - Revenues Team Leader — 3 FTE
      - Revenues Officer — 36 FTE
      - Visiting Officer — 4.69 FTE
      - Modern Apprentice — 4.0 FTE
  - Revenues and Assessments Manager — 1 FTE
    - Assessment Team Leader — 10.5 FTE
      - Assessment Officer — 58 FTE
      - Customer Services Assistant — 16.56 FTE
      - Recovery Officers — 6 FTE
      - Modern Apprentice — 1 FTE
    - Revenues & Assessments Assistants — 23.66 FTE
  - Revenues & Assessment Manager — 1 FTE
    - Technical Officers (Revenues & Assessments) — 2 FTE
      - Assessment QA Officer — 1 FTE
      - Revenues QA Officer — 1 FTE
    - Systems Team Leader — 1 FTE
      - Systems Support Officers — 3.80 FTE
      - Systems Administrators — 2 FTE
        - Modern Apprentice — 1.0 FTE

*Structure current as at 18/03/2019

27

EXHIBIT D

Reference Number: FOI 101004484955

Response provided under: Freedom of Information Act 2000

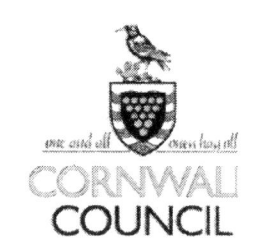

Request:

Please provide me with the following information under the Freedom of Information Act 2000.

Will you please send me the salaries of all the named job titles on the customer services flow chart which you supplied me.

Response:

Please find below a table detailing the salary ranges for the posts previously provided to you in response to your FOI request 101004430152.

Post	Grade	Salary Range £ per annum
Head of Revenues & Assessment	Q	68,529 - 83,753
Revenues and Assessment Manager	L	37,935 – 45,591
Revenues Team Leader	I	24,590 – 31,371
Assessment Team Leader	I	24,590 – 31,371
Revenues & Assessment Team Leader (Systems)	I	24,590 – 31,371
Court Officer	H	21,623 -26,317
Technical Officer (Revenues and Assessment)	H	21,623 -26,317
System Administrator	H	21,623 -26,317
Revenues Officer	G	19,331 -23,836
Assessment Officer	G	19,331 -23,836
Recovery Officer	G	19,331 -23,836
Assessment Quality Assurance Officer	G	19,331 -23,836
Revenues Quality Assurance Officer	G	19,331 -23,836
Systems Support Officer	G	19,331 -23,836
Visiting Officer	H	21,623 -26,317
Customer Service Assistant	F	17,364 -21,166
Revenues & Assessment	E	17,364 -18,797

Assistant		
Modern Apprentice	Level 2	£11,684*
	Level 3	£15,839**

Information provided by: Customer Access and Digital Services (Revenues)

Date of response: 14 June 2019

EXHIBIT E

Reference Number: FOI 101004420840

Response provided under: Freedom of Information Act 2000

Request:
Please provide me with the following information under the Freedom of Information Act 2000.

I am requesting a breakdown of payments made on Credit Card from Cornwall Council to HMCTS 2018 - 2019:

1. The set fee for the summons;

2. The set fee for liability orders;

3. The quarterly payments for magistrate's expenses;

4 The fee for hiring the room as a venue from HMCTS;

Plus, Cornwall Council's expenses of;

5. Printing summonses and liability orders;

6. Costs of postage;

7. Labour costs.

Response:

1. The set fee for the summons up to the 25 July 2018 was £3.00. After the 25 July 2018, the set fee for the summons is £0.50p
2. The set fee for a liability order is £20.00
3. We do not hold any information regarding Magistrates expenses.
4. There is no fee for the hiring of the venue
5. The cost of printing summonses for 2018/2019 is £1,244.65. We do not print liability orders
6. The cost of posting the summonses in 2018/2019 is £8,961.48
7. Labour costs involved for the above in 2018/2019 is £1,826,320.00

Information provided by: Customer Access and Digital Services (Revenues)

EXHIBIT F

22/06/2019   Cornwall Council

In the case of Cheney-v-Conn (Inspector of Taxes) (1968), Mr Justice Ungoed-Thomas stated at page 782 'I shall mention another limb to the tax payers argument, namely, that any unlawful purpose for which a statutory enactment may be made vitiates the enforcement of that statute. As was pointed out by the Crown, if that argument was correct, it would mean that the supremacy of Parliament would, in effect be over ruled. If the purpose of which a statute may be used is an invalid purpose and not to invalidate in the statute itself. What the statute itself enacts cannot be unlawful, because what the statue says and provides is itself the law, and the highest form of law that is known to this country. It is the law which prevails over every other form of law, and it is not for the court to say that a parliamentary enactment, the highest law in this country, is illegal. Therefore, the courts have confirmed that statutes over rule common law and statutory provisions are enforceable by the courts.

I would therefore strongly advise you to contact the council tax section on 0300 12341 171 to discuss a suitable payment arrangement, if you are not in a position to pay the debt in full.

The total court costs added to council tax accounts where a summons has been issued and a liability order is obtained is £80.00.

Please see the table below for the calculation of these costs.

Summons	Description	Cost
	Production, printing, packing & posting	£2.23
	Admin	£55.46
Liability Order	**Description**	**Cost**
	Production, printing, packing & posting	£2.23
	Admin	£18.60
Court Fee		£3.00
	Total	**£81.52**

Please note that we are required to reach agreement with the Magistrates' Court on the amount of the costs we add to council tax accounts in addition to the £3.00 court fee, and the above amounts have been agreed by the Court.

EXHIBIT G

HMCTS_BLK_DIGI

https://www.gov.uk/government/organisations/hm-courts-and-tribunals-service/about/personal-information-charter

From: Sutton Julia [mailto:julia.sutton@cornwall.gov.uk]
Sent: 27 March 2019 12:38
To: cornwall-list <cornwall-list@Justice.gov.uk>
Subject: Complaint list and total for c/tax and NDR for 18th April 2019 court at Bodmin

Hi

Please find attached the Cornwall Council Complaint lists to be signed and authorised for the court hearing at Bodmin court on 18th April 2019.

We are laying before you today complaint lists for a total of 1136 x Council Tax summonses and 56 x NDR summonses issued for this court.

It is time critical that we have confirmation that the list has been signed, as we have to get the summons letters in the post by close of business today or tomorrow at the latest.

Please can you email:-

Adrian Walters – Adrian.Walters@cornwall.gov.uk (01209 614103),

Lynda Ryan – lryan@cornwall.gov.uk (01872 224754)

Julia Sutton – Julia.Sutton@cornwall.gov.uk to confirm that the lists have been signed.

Thanks

Julia

Julia Sutton | Revenues Assistant

Cornwall Council | Customer Access and Digital Service

Julia.Sutton@cornwall.gov.uk | Tel: 01872 327095 | Internal Number: 497095

From: DeMenezes, Raul On Behalf Of cwll-legal
Sent: 27 March 2019 13:52
To: cornwall-list <cornwall-list@Justice.gov.uk>
Subject: RE: Complaint list and total for c/tax and NDR for 18th April 2019 court at Bodmin

Authorised

RdeM

From: Wearne, Carli On Behalf Of cornwall-list
Sent: 27 March 2019 12:54
To: cwll-legal <cwll-legal@Justice.gov.uk>
Subject: FW: Complaint list and total for c/tax and NDR for 18th April 2019 court at Bodmin

Good afternoon,

Please find attached Council Tax and NDR complaints for checking and authorisation please.

Many thanks,

Carli

Mrs C Wearne

Administration/Listing Officer

Cornwall Magistrates' Court | HMCTS | Launceston Road | Bodmin | PL31 2AL

Phone: 01208 262700

Working days – Wednesday, Thursday, Friday

19

cid:image001.jpg@01D23B57.EBA26E10

From: Tonkin, Penelope [mailto:penelope.tonkin@Justice.gov.uk] On Behalf Of cornwall-list
Sent: 27 March 2019 14:05
To: Walters Adrian; Sutton Julia
Subject: Complaint list and total for c/tax and NDR for 18th April 2019 court at Bodmin

Good afternoon,

Thank you for your email.

The complaint list for the 18th April 2019, before Bodmin Magistrates' Court has been authorised.

Kind regards,

Penny

Penny Tonkin

Administration Officer

Cornwall Magistrates' Court | HMCTS | Launceston Road | Bodmin | PL31 2AL

Phone: 01208 262723 Internal: 8332 2723

Here is how HMCTS uses personal data about you.

HMCTS_BLK_DIGI

RE: summons
Wed, 12 Jun 2019 13:19
cornwall-admin (cornwall-admin@Justice.gov.uk)
To:you Details
Dear Mr Patterson

Your email below has been referred to a court Legal Adviser, who has instructed me to reply as follows:

The information given is correct. Even though the Justices Clerks did not personally consider the summons in each case their functions would have been delegated to the Legal Advisers who consider them. The letter does state that the reference to the Justices Clerk includes a Legal Adviser. The Court is satisfied that the requirement under the law has been met in each case, and suggests that you may raise this and anything else when you next appear before the court.

Regards

Mr Rutherford

Administrative Officer

Cornwall Magistrates Court | HMCTS | The Law Courts, Launceston Road | Bodmin | PL31 2AL

Phone: 01208 262700

I am not authorised to bind my Department contractually, not to make representations or other statements which may bind the Department in any way via electronic means.

ü Protect our environment - save paper - do you need to print this email?

From: Paul Patterson [mailto:paulstroketalk@aol.com]
Sent: 09 June 2019 13:36
To: cornwall-admin <cornwall-admin@Justice.gov.uk>
Subject: Re: summons

EXHIBIT I

IN THE COUNTY OF CORNWALL LOCAL JUSTICE AREA OF EAST CORNWALL

SUMMONS FOR NON-PAYMENT OF COUNCIL TAX

MR PAUL PATTERSON
2 TREMAYNE TERRACE
WIDEGATES
LOOE
CORNWALL
PL13 1QW

Summons No: 179339
Account Reference: 313359998
Property Reference No: 11164182002000

Complaint has this day been made to me, the undersigned, by Cornwall Council, that you, being a person duly taxed and assessed for Council Tax, have not paid the sum(s) shown below.

Council Tax set on	Address giving rise to the charge	Period of charge	Balance O/S
20.02.2018	2 TREMAYNE TERRACE WIDEGATES LOOE PL13 1QW	01.04.2018 to 31.03.2019	£853.05

Total Council Tax Outstanding	£853.05
Summons Costs	£57.50
TOTAL AMOUNT DUE	**£910.55**

You are hereby summoned to appear:

on **18 April 2019**
at **1:30 p.m.**
before the Magistrates Court sitting at **LAUNCESTON ROAD BODMIN CORNWALL PL31 2AL**

to show cause why you have not paid the said total sum. If you do not appear you will be proceeded against as if you had appeared and be dealt with according to the law.

The granting of a Liability Order will result in additional costs of £20.00 being incurred.

Dated: 26.03.2019   Signed:

Clerk to the Justices

Please see reverse for ways to pay and Cornwall Council contact information.
If the amount of Council Tax outstanding and costs are paid to Cornwall Council before the date of the court hearing all further proceedings in respect of this summons will be stopped.

The legal notice dated 22nd June 2019 can be downloaded from: -
https://drive.google.com/file/d/1mKnl7HRxC2GTFeJvEQgnKRD_AIecp2Cg/view?usp=sharing

The council's costs have to be costs reasonably 'incurred' Five pounds costs may seem reasonable, but if the actual costs incurred was only two pounds, then the five pound would not have been reasonable incurred. This is what I believe Judge Baker failed to see, or didn't want to see in dismissing my case. So I applied for a case to be stated.

CHAPTER 3

APPLICATION TO STATE A CASE

Paul Patterson

2 Tremayne Terrace Widegates Looe Cornwall

LEGAL NOTICE

16th July 2019

Cornwall Council Acct Ref 313359998

Bodmin Magistrates' Court

THE JUSTICES' CHIEF EXECUTIVE

THE MAGISTRATES' COURT

BODMIN

Application to state a case to Appeal - pursuant to section 111 of the Magistrates' Court Act 1980

RE: Council Tax liability order application Thursday 27th June 2019

RE: Questions for the opinion of the High Court – ref liability order costs for council tax

Dear Mr. Martyn Stephens,

I am contacting you in relation to the Court sitting on Thursday 27th June 2019 heard an application for liability order and costs against me on application by Cornwall Council in respect on non-payment of council tax. The case followed the issue of summonses under the Council Tax (Administration & Enforcement) Regulations 1992 SI 613. I am concerned that there was a procedural error made during this event and also that certain key information was not properly considered.

Accordingly, I hereby apply under section 111 of the Magistrates' Court Act 1980; set out my questions to the Court sitting in the above proceeding to state a case for the High Court.

The questions for the opinion of the (Administrative) High Court are as follows:

In respect of the application for liability order for granted by the Cornwall Council on Thursday June 27th 2019 for non-payment of council tax; I wish the court and justices to investigate and confirm the following 3 questions;

1

During the procedure the district judge Mrs. Baker heard my evidence; but I was not offered nor invited to do so under Oath; yet the other party from Cornwall Council – *Mr Adrian Walters's* evidence was given 'under oath'? On what basis in law does the court allow only the applicant to give evidence under oath and not the defendant? I believe this single point of law has therefore bias and prejudiced my case as the district judge Mrs. Baker clearly did not listen nor consider a word written or spoken that I delivered.

District judge stated she was not considering the labour costs but the overall hidden costs, this is where the district judged erred as the council's so called hidden costs are calculated in their expenses; which she failed [refused] to see. District judge failed to see that the council is inflating their costs by stating that their labour costs to complete summonses are more time consuming than they really are. The council's costs and calculations clearly show this, as well as the evidence in my legal notice. By doing this they are also inflating their expenses, as expenses are calculated to be 39.4% of their labour costs.

District judge Mrs. Baker erred in-law by failing to listen or consider page 11 of my legal notice dated 22nd June 2019 on how the costs of £77.50 was computed (Cornwall Council's costs and calculations) The council clearly state in their costs and calculations that 60.6% of their costs are labour while 39.4% are all other expenses.

The district judge stated during the hearing that it could be said that the council's cost are too low, this remark should never have been made, as the judge cannot add on costs and expenses which the council are not claiming for, only costs reasonably incurred.

2

Again; no financial means test was completed by the council; or the court; this is the fourth liability order in a row for me – yet no financial means test has been done; if no financial means test is done; then the liability order becomes effectively void for committal purposes.

On what basis in law does the court or council believe that the issuing of an LO without a financial means test taken at the time; when it cannot be enforced by the LA [or any court] to show and prove to a 'criminal standard' *culpable neglect* nor *willful refusal*?

Any committal proceedings now taken by the council would be unlawful, unreasonable, unjust and unconscionable.

3

On what basis in law does the Court allow a direct breach of the Bangalore Principles of holding a court; that the court is neither impartial nor independent as it is being paid by the council for the hiring of the room; costs of the justices, summons and orders?

The facts are that this is a NON HMCTS Procedure; which is a civil matter brought by the local authority in bulk every 2 weeks where there are no CPR rules within the procedure and no disclosed subject matter jurisdiction that these 'hearings' have lawful authority and are not a clear breach of human rights article 6 – right to a fair trial. Can the court also confirm if a Liability order is a 'Court order'?

I would be most grateful if the Court can formulate the case for the opinion of the High Court as soon as practicable because of the importance of the issues involved.

Please let me know when the draft case is completed. I wait to hear from you.

Yours faithfully,

District judge Dian Baker refused to state a case.

CHAPTER 4

REFUSAL TO STATE A CASE

IN THE CORNWALL MAGISTRATES' COURT

CERTIFICATE OF REFUSAL TO STATE A CASE

(Magistrates' Courts Act 1980, s 111(5)). – Cornwall Magistrates' Court. On the 27th June 2019 a complaint was preferred by an officer of Cornwall Council against Mr Paul Patterson that he should be made the subject of a liability order in relation to unpaid council tax and was determined by me as described in the annexes to this certificate.
The said Mr Patterson being aggrieved by the determination as being wrong in law has applied to me to state a case for the opinion of the High Court.

I am of the opinion that the application is frivolous and so refuse to state a case.
Dated the 5th day of August 2019

District Judge (Magistrates' Courts) Diana Baker
2 of 9
Annex A

History

On 27th June 2019 Mr Paul Patterson appeared before the Cornwall Magistrates' Court at Bodmin in relation to council tax enforcement proceedings.
A more detailed history of the case is set out in the judgement that I delivered that day and which is attached to this certificate at annex B for the benefit of the reader.

On 27th June I ordered:
(i) a liability order against Mr Patterson, in accordance with his concession that he was unable to avail himself of any of the defences to the making of such an order; and (ii) that Mr Patterson is to pay £77.50 costs to Cornwall Council.
On 17th July, My Patterson submitted to the court by email an application to me to state a case for the opinion of the High Court, pursuant to section 111 of the Magistrates' Courts Act 1980.

The application
The rules surrounding the submission of an application under section 111 are set out at part 35 of the Criminal Procedure Rules.
The application purports to set out three questions for the opinion of the High Court, though I observe that the suggested questions are a combination of questions, assertions and representations.
I do not replicate the application here, but I append it to this certificate at annex C.
It is not clear to me that the applicant has served upon Cornwall Council a copy of his application in accordance with r.35.2(b)(ii). However, suffice it to say that I have not received any representations on the application.

Reasons for refusal to state a case

As certificated above, I refuse to state a case for the opinion of the High Court on the grounds that this application is frivolous.

I reach the conclusion that this application is frivolous on the following grounds:

(i) Any suggestion that I erred in law in the making of a liability order is completely without merit. The defences to the making of a liability order are limited. They were explained to Mr Patterson, who conceded that he was unable to avail himself of any of those defences. It followed that I was required in law to make the order;

(ii) Mr Patterson complains that I heard evidence from Mr Walters of Cornwall Council on oath, but that he was not given the opportunity to be sworn himself before addressing me. Mr Patterson has misunderstood the procedure. At the hearing on the 27th June I told Mr Patterson that, as part 3 of 9 of the process of applying for the liability order, the council must be sworn because I was required to be satisfied on evidence in relation to various procedural grounds prior to the making of the liability order.

The making of the liability order having been conceded by Mr Patterson, I was not required to hear evidence from him.

After dealing with the liability order I was required to consider the issue of costs, which was contested. It was at this stage that I heard representations from both the local authority and Mr Patterson.

This was explained to Mr Patterson on the day and it follows that this ground of the application to state a case is completely without merit;

(iii) Mr Patterson complains that I erred in law as I failed to consider his legal notice, in particular, page 11. This is simply not true. I did consider it and I explained that when I delivered the reasons for my decision in court. Mr Patterson helpfully provided me with a well-researched and detailed document in advance of the hearing, which set out his arguments. I considered that document along with its schedules and Mr Patterson's representations prior to making my decision in the matter. The suggestion that I did not is groundless;

(iv) Mr Patterson suggests that I commented during the course of the hearing that 'it could be said that the council's costs are too low'. What I actually remarked is that I deal with a number of cases concerning council tax and that costs can vary, be they higher or lower, from one local authority to the next. This does not amount to an error of law and cannot be a ground for stating a case;

(v) Mr Patterson queries the legality of the making of a liability order without first conducting a financial means test. However, the law is clear and does not permit me to conduct a means test as part of liability order proceedings and it follows that this is not a ground for stating a case.

(vi) Finally, Mr Patterson queries the fairness of his hearing. I conducted Mr Patterson's hearing in the proper way, in open court, during the course of which both parties had the opportunity to address me at length on the merits of the case. Mr Patterson's suggestion that I was neither impartial nor independent in these proceedings is entirely without merit or substance and is not a ground for stating a case.

Dated the 5th day of August 2019
District Judge (Magistrates' Courts) Diana Baker

Annex B
CORNWALL COUNCIL v Patterson

Mr Patterson has received a liability order summons for non-payment of Council Tax. He has objected to that application and made various requests to the court and the Council to verify the validity of the summons on application.
His case was adjourned from the 10th April 2019 to the 29th May 2019.
On the 12th June 2019 Mr Rutherford from the administration team emailed Mr Patterson stating that a legal adviser had considered his representations and the summons had been lawfully issued.

An email dated the 17th April 2019 to Mr Patterson sets out clearly the procedure and law in relation to the issue of Council Tax summonses and I can confirm that the advice given in that email is correct.
I had understood the only issue to be raised today was the granting of the liability order and in particular the costs the Council were applying for in relation to that application.

Mr Patterson in his "Legal Notice" dated 22nd June 2019 again reiterates his arguments in relation to the lawfulness of the issue of the original summons. I have referred him back to the email of the 17th April 2019 and can confirm that the Court is satisfied that the summons was properly issued. Mr De Menezes has delegated powers issued to him by Mr Roveri. He does not need to personally sign the document. I turn now to the grant of a liability order.

Regulation 34 of the Council Tax (Administration and Enforcement) Regulations 1992 sets out the provisions for a billing authority to apply to a Magistrates' court for a liability order for non-payment of Council Tax. The regulations provide that if the amount which has fallen due and which has been subject to a reminder notice or final notice remains wholly or partly unpaid on expiry of the conditions of the reminder or final notice, the billing authority can apply to the court for a liability order.

The defences available against the granting of a liability order are very limited. These are that:
1. there is no entry in relation to the dwelling in the valuation list.
2. the Council Tax has not been properly set.
3. the Council Tax has not been demanded in accordance with the statutory provisions.
4. the amount demanded has been paid.
5. More than 6 years has elapsed since the day on which the sum became due.
6. The sum outstanding is in respect of a penalty which is the subject of an appeal on arbitration.
7. Bankruptcy or winding up proceedings have been initiated.
These are the only defences. The Court cannot consider any personal circumstances of Mr Patterson at this stage. Therefore, Mr Patterson cannot avail himself of any of the above defences and he now concedes this so the court will make the order.

I will turn to Mr Patterson's argument regarding the costs. I am grateful to him for providing me with a well-researched and detailed document setting out his argument and providing me with the costs disclosure schedules.

The regulations allow payment of costs of a sum equal to the costs reasonably incurred by the applicant in obtaining the order (regulation 34(7)).

Mr Patterson says that the Court should not grant the Council's application for costs as it has never carried out any calculation of the Council's costs. As I have explained to Mr Patterson, this is not for the Court to do, it only has to be satisfied the costs are reasonable in the circumstances.

He maintains the costs orders are being used as a penalty and are made to cover general costs of collecting Council Tax. He explains that Magistrates have been approving costs for production, printing, packaging posting of liability orders which in fact are not printed.

Mr Patterson helpfully refers me to the case of Nicholson v Tottenham Magistrates' Court which gives the court guidance on the approach to be taken in these cases. It confirms that the Court must be satisfied that the local authority has actually incurred the costs. The costs in question were incurred in obtaining the liability order and it was reasonable for the Council to incur them. That case makes it clear that it would be impermissible to apply for costs that in fact relate to the overall administration of Council Tax in the area concerned, however, it is permissible to include administration costs, legal fees and out of pocket expenses generally attributable to the enforcement process in obtaining a liability order. When looking at the costs schedules, I do not need to be satisfied each revenue officer or other officer incurred the specific amounts in each case. I simply consider whether the costs are reasonable. To help with that I take into account the detailed evidence of what work goes into the making of each application.

To be in a position to apply for a liability order the Council needs to be sure for each individual summoned that that person has a valid account, that the appropriate sum has been requested, that the reminder notices have been served and that the amount remains unpaid. We have heard of all the checks that are made by the revenue officer.

They then have to collate all the information as their representative has to give that information on oath to the Court. They need to liaise with the Court office to arrange for any summonses to be considered. Sometimes this is a slow process but at other times it is longer. They need to print off the summons for the Court, print off the full 6 of 9 schedule and check all of them prior to the application in case any are paid. This is a time-consuming process. The officers then need to post all the summonses, attend Court and make the applications.

If granted an individual would need to be notified and notices sent by post. In running a Council department there are not just the administrative officers to take into account but there must also include regulatory, supervision and salaries to take into account the overall costs.

I am satisfied all this has been done on Mr Patterson's account. The Council are requesting £77.50 and sets out in its disclosure to Mr Patterson how it comes to that figure. It accepts it does not print liability orders but if granted it does print a letter confirming the grant of the order. It accepts there are no senior enforcement officers but that reference refers to experienced officers who receive greater pay.

Prior to the making of any costs application it is good practice to agree the amount of costs asked for with the local court.

The Council confirm this was done.

Such an agreement is normal practice but it does not preclude any individual (as Mr Patterson is lawfully doing) making an application to the Court questioning its reasonableness.

I have carefully considered Mr Patterson's representations and the representations and costs schedule from the Council.

I again reiterate, I am not looking at whether each amount in the schedule has been spent on Mr Patterson's case. I am asking myself whether the costs applied for have actually been incurred in obtaining the liability order and whether it was entirely reasonable for the Council to incur them. I am so satisfied on all counts.

I therefore grant the Council's application for a Liability order and I grant £77.50 costs on the liability order.

I confirm that now the Court has fully considered the reasonableness of the costs incurred, the Court will not hear any further applications challenging the lawfulness of the cost unless an applicant is able to distinguish their case from the findings made in this case.

I do not consider it appropriate to grant any further costs in this application for today's hearing and for the file preparation for today's hearing.

Mr Patterson is following a democratic process in that it is his right to challenge the reasonableness of the of the costs and in doing so the Council now have a definitive decision on the reasonableness.

Dated this 27th day of June 2019

It's clear from Judge Baker's comments that she has allowed the council to claim costs which they have never 'incurred.'

So after receiving this refusal to have a case stated I sent an application to have the case judicially reviewed.

CHAPTER 5

APPLICATION FOR JUDICIAL REVIEW

IN THE HIGH COURT OF JUSTICE   Claim No;

QUEEN'S BENCH DIVISION

Royal Courts of Justice
Strand, London, WC2A 2LL

Date: 08/08/2019

Between:

The Queen on the application of;

MR PAUL D. PATTERSON   Appellant

And

CORNWALL MAGISTRATES COURT (E1)   Respondent

CORNWALL COUNCIL   Interested Party

INDEX

PAGE 3   SKELETON ARGUMENT

PAGE 4   STATEMENT OF GROUNDS

PAGE 5   **EXHIBIT 1** The order certificate dated 05 08 2019

PAGE 6   **EXHIBIT 2** Grounds for refusing to state a case

PAGE 8   **EXHIBIT 3** Application to state a case dated 16th July 2019

PAGE 9   **EXHIBIT 4** Legal Noticed dated 22nd June 2019

PAGE 15   **EXHIBIT 5** Rev Paul Nicolson

SKELETON ARGUMENT

This application is to have the following order reviewed;

The order [certificate dated 05 08 2019 **EXHIBIT 1**] to refuse to a state case via way of appeal by Cornwall Magistrates Court is void as an error in law as a grounds for refusing to state a case [**EXHIBIT 2**] were unreasonable and also for the following lawful reasons;

1. That the Court allowed unlawful and unjustified costs added to the application.

2. The Appellant claims the Council has breached High Court Case ruling of: CO/976/2014

Rev Paul Nicholson v Tottenham Magistrates EXHIBIT 5, because adding unreasonable costs to claim was unlawful.

STATEMENT OF GROUNDS

Point 1

The court allowed the council £77.50 in costs per liability Order made; it was clear from the councils own calculations provided **EXHIBIT 4** page 11 that these costs are highly inflated. The council admits **EXHIBIT 4** page 12 that, "We do not employ staff for the sole purpose of Council Tax recovery work. Multi skilled officers within the Revenues and Assessment team are involved in the daily administration of recovery work, in addition to processing other Revenues & Assessment work." The council's own calculations show that the council would need to employ a team of FULL-TIME staff for the sole purpose of Council Tax recovery.

The District judge Mrs. Baker appears to have confused the reasonableness of the *amount* of the costs with the question whether that sum was reasonably *incurred*.

Point 2

It is clear from the appellants legal notice dated 22nd June 2019 **[EXHIBIT 4]** that the council's costs are highly inflated, that they are being used as a means of covering the council's general administrative costs of collecting council tax, rather than reflecting any actual or fair appraisal of the actual costs incurred.

<u>District judge Mrs. Baker stated she was not considering the labour costs but the overall hidden costs, this is where the district judged erred as the council's so called hidden costs are calculated in their expenses; which she failed [refused] to see.</u>

<u>District judge failed to see that the council is inflating their costs by stating that their labour costs to complete summonses are more time consuming than they really are.</u>

<u>The council's costs and calculations clearly show this, as well as the evidence in my legal notice. By doing this they are also inflating their expenses, as expenses are calculated to be 39.4% of their labour costs.</u>

The appellant pointed out to the court that the council's cost for the liability order of £20.00 was different from other local authorities giving the example of Lambeth being only £5.00 The judge replied that that was of no concern to this court.

It must be remembered that summonses and liability order notices are sent to despondents by post using computer-generated standard letters, by the press of a button.

Quite interesting when you compare it with what was said in the Nicholson case.

District judge Mrs. Baker stated;

"Mr Patterson says that the Court should not grant the Council's application for costs as it has never carried out any calculation of the Council's costs. As I have explained to Mr Patterson, this is not for the Court to do, it only has to be satisfied the costs are reasonable in the circumstances."

In the Rev Paul Nicolson case the Judge stated,

"i) the Magistrates did not have sufficient relevant information before them to reach a proper judicial determination of whether the costs claimed represented costs reasonably incurred by the Council in obtaining the liability order;

ii) the Magistrates erred in law by failing to make further inquiries into how the £125 was computed and what elements it comprised"

Yours Faithfully,

Paul D. Patterson.

My application to apply for a judicial review was sent within the 90-day time limit from the date of the refusal to state a case. My application was returned to me stating that as I was asking for help with fees, I had to send further information of my means, bank and tax returns. So I had to send a fresh application, once again sending 3 judicial review claim forms (N461) 3 bundle of documents and the form (EX160 help with fees.)

After some time once again all my documents where returned to me, this time they stated that I had only sent them 2 pages of the 6 page claim forms, and that I had to send in a new application. So for a third time I sent in my application explaining to the court that this delay is now making my application out of time. I felt this was a deliberate way of dismissing my case.

In the High Court of Justice
Queen's Bench Division
Administrative Court

CO Ref: CO/8/2020

In the matter of an application for Judicial Review

The Queen on the application of **PAUL D PATTERSON**

versus **CORNWALL MAGISTRATES' COURT** (Defendant)

and **CORNWALL COUNCIL** (Interested Party)

Application for permission to apply for Judicial Review
NOTIFICATION of the Judge's decision (CPR Part 54.11, 54.12)

Following consideration of the documents lodged by the Claimant and the Acknowledgements of service filed by the Defendant and Interested Party

Order by the Honourable Mr Justice SUPPERSTONE

Permission is hereby REFUSED; the application is considered to be totally without merit

Reasons:

1. On 27 June 2019 the Claimant appeared before DJ Baker at Cornwall Magistrates' Court in relation to council tax enforcement proceedings. The judge made a liability order against the Claimant, in accordance with his concession that he was unable to avail himself of any of the defences to the making of such an order, and ordered that the Claimant pay £77.50 costs to Cornwall Council.

2. The Claimant now seeks to challenge the decision of the District Judge made on 27 June 2019 (certificate handed down on 5 August 2019) not to state a case for the opinion of the High Court.

3. The Claim Form was filed out of time on 30 December 2019. The Claimant has made no application for an extension of time other than to state in section 8 of the Claim Form that he wishes to make an application for "Help with fees". Although he is a litigant in person he knows of the time limit rules. In 2018 in the case of *R (Paul D Patterson) v Cornwall Magistrates' Court and Cornwall Council* (CO/506/2018) HH Judge Blair QC, sitting as a deputy High Court judge, refused him permission to apply for judicial review because, inter alia, the application was out of time, stating "an application for judicial review must be filed 'promptly'. The absolute maximum time limit for applying for a judicial review is 3 months". The judge refused to grant an extension of time, stating "finding out about getting help with the Issue Fee is not a sufficient basis for granting an extension of time to file the claim".

4. In any event, none of the grounds of challenge are arguable. The grounds disclose no arguable error of law. I consider the sum of costs awarded of £77.50 to be a reasonable sum. In his decision dated 5 August 2019 the DJ explains why he refused to state a case, which includes the reasons for the costs order. In giving his decision on liability and costs on 27 June 2019 the judge considered the representations from the parties and the costs schedule from the Defendant. The judge stated he considered the reasonableness of the costs involved. In the circumstances on 5 August 2019 the judge considered the application to state a case to be totally frivolous. I agree.

5. For the reasons I have given, I also consider this claim to be totally without merit.

BY VIRTUE OF CPR 54.12(7) THE CLAIMANT MAY NOT REQUEST THAT THE DECISION TO REFUSE PERMISSION BE RECONSIDERED AT A HEARING.

Signed: *Michael Supperstone*   Date: 10 February 2020

The date of service of this order is calculated from the date in the section below

12 FEB 2020

It is clear these judges are closing their eyes to the fact that Cornwall Council are claiming for costs which they have not 'incurred.'

I wrote to Cornwall Council asking who were these Revenue and Finance officers involved with calculating the council summons costs, and they refused to name the officers.

If these officers are committing fraud they should be named.

Dear Mr Patterson,

Thank you for your enquiry regarding the calculation of summons costs and I apologise for the delay in replying.

Information relating to individuals has been withheld under Section 40 (2) (Personal information) of the Act.

Section 40 (2) applies where disclosure of third party personal information would breach any of the Data Protection principles.

The Council has a legal requirement under the Data Protection Act 2018 ("DPA") to process personal data fairly and lawfully. The Council considers that releasing third party personal information would be unfair and that such a disclosure would breach Principle One of the DPA.

Yours sincerely,

Adrian Walters.

The Council Tax (Administration and Enforcement) Regulations 1992

Application for liability order
34 –7 (b) a sum of an amount equal to the costs **reasonably incurred** by the applicant in obtaining the order.
https://www.legislation.gov.uk/uksi/1992/613/regulation/34/made

The above regulation is one, which all local authorities are breaking, they are all highly inflating their costs which is fraudulent, deceitful and unlawful.

CHAPTER 6

HULL CITY COUNCIL

PAUL PATTERSON made this Freedom of Information request **to Hull City Council**

A breakdown of costs & calculations claimed for council tax summonses approved by magistrates.

https://www.whatdotheyknow.com/request/a_breakdown_of_costs_calculation#outgoing-1017294

Dear Kingston upon Hull City Council,
Please can you supply me with copies of your breakdown of the costs and calculations approved by the Magistrates, which the council has claimed for council tax summonses 2018-2019, 2019- 2020.

Yours faithfully,

PAUL PATTERSON

Information Governance, Hull City Council 9 March 2020
Dear Mr Patterson

Freedom of Information Act 2000 – Information Request - 000327/20

With regard to your Freedom of Information request received on 10 February 2020, please find our response below.

Q

Please can you supply me with copies of your breakdown of the costs and calculations approved by the Magistrates which the council have claimed for council tax summonses 2018-2019, 2019- 2020.

A

For the answer to this question please refer to the table below:

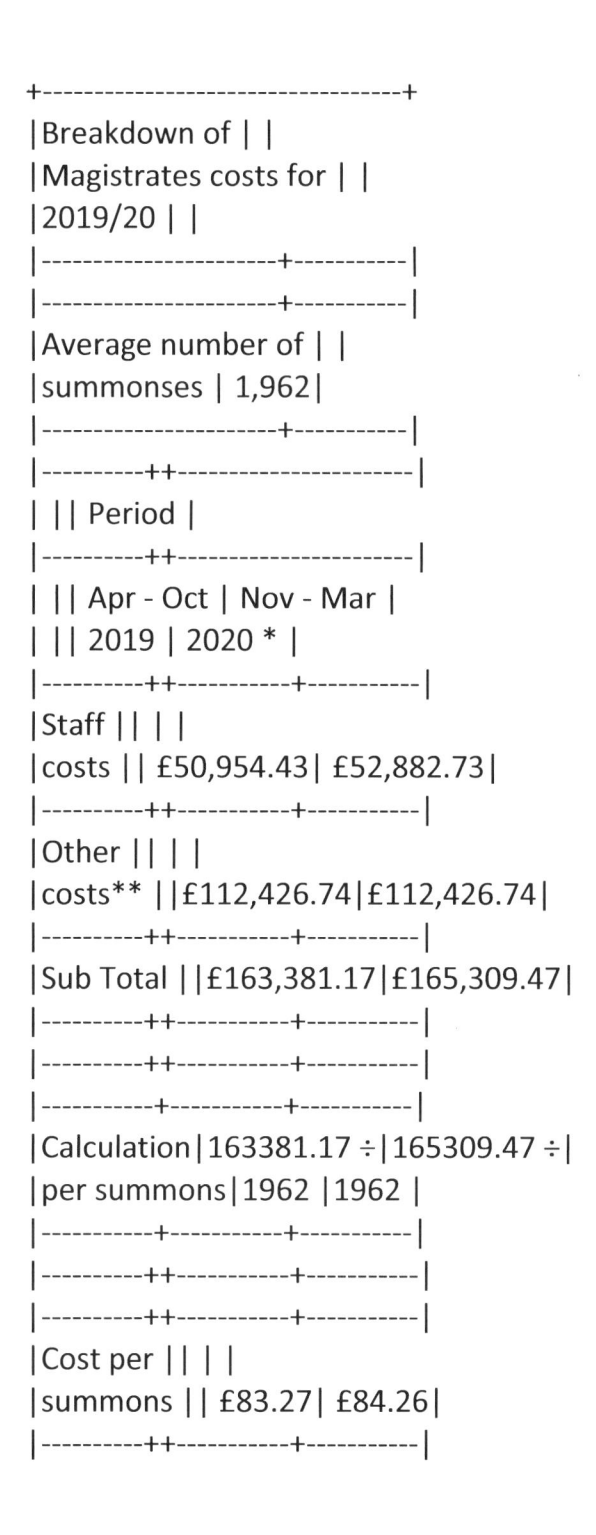

Breakdown of Magistrates costs for 2019/20		
Average number of summonses	1,962	
	Period	
	Apr - Oct 2019	Nov - Mar 2020 *
Staff costs	£50,954.43	£52,882.73
Other costs**	£112,426.74	£112,426.74
Sub Total	£163,381.17	£165,309.47
Calculation per summons	163381.17 ÷ 1962	165309.47 ÷ 1962
Cost per summons	£83.27	£84.26

```
|Court fee || £0.50| £0.50|
|----------++-----------+----------|
|Total || £83.77| £84.76|
+----------------------------------+
```

*Includes 2% Civica pay increase

**Figures includes costs for Customer service support, internal recharges, IT, premises, printing and non-court fees.

We hope that you will be satisfied with our response and should you require any further information then please do not hesitate to contact us.

Should you wish to complain about our response in any way this must initially be done by e-mailing [1][Hull City Council request email] or by contacting us at The Information Governance Team, The Guildhall, Alfred Gelder Street, Hull, HU1 2AA.

If you are not satisfied with the outcome of the internal review then you may take your complaint to the Information Commissioner's Office, the government body established to enforce the legislation.

Information Commissioner's Office

Wycliffe House Water Lane,

Wilmslow,

Cheshire,

SK9 5AF

PAUL PATTERSON 9 March 2020

Dear Information Governance,

This breakdown of costs is not detailed enough. Can you please give me a breakdown of the staffing labour costs @minutes allocated per summons and liability order per officer.

Yours sincerely,

PAUL PATTERSON.

PAUL PATTERSON 9 March 2020

Dear Information Governance,

Can you also give a breakdown of:
1. Other |costs £112,426.74|£112,426.74
2. What are all of these other costs?
A council can only lawfully charge for costs incurred for the sending out of summonses and the granting of the order. I notice the council is claiming for Customer service support, this has nothing to do with the costs incurred for summonses and the granting of liability orders.
4. How much is being claimed for Customer service support?

Yours sincerely,

PAUL PATTERSON.

Dear Mr Patterson

Freedom of Information Act 2000 – Information Request - 000327/20

Further to our e-mail of 9 March please accept our apologies for the delay in providing our response attached and below.

Q

This breakdown of costs is not detailed enough. Can you please give me a breakdown of the staffing labour costs @minutes allocated per summons and liability order per officer.

A

In accordance with Section 17 of the Freedom of Information Act, the Council is required to inform you that some of the information on the enclosed document has not been provided and has been withheld due to the following exemption under the Act.

Section 43 - Commercial interests

It is considered that disclosure of these costs could prejudice the commercial interests of Civica and the Council.

Applies to the information you have requested in regard to staff costs for Civica employees. Disclosure of information is prohibited when it would or be likely to prejudice the commercial interests of the company (including the public authority holding it).

We have considered the public interest in regard to the release of these staff costs and in so doing have weighed the benefits that disclosure would provide in respect of openness and accountability against the harm and prejudice which could be caused to the current provider of Council Tax and Housing benefit services to the authority. We believe that in this case release of these costs could compromise the commercial interests of Civica and could harm the Council's reputation in any other future contract negotiations. We therefore believe in this case there is not enough justification to release the information and the public interest in with holding the information outweighs the public interest in disclosure. Where this exemption has been applied the figures have been replaced with 'S43' accordingly.

Should you require any further information then please do not hesitate to contact us.

Although information supplied in response to your request may be in Microsoft Excel format please feel free to contact us should you wish the information to be supplied in an alternative more readable/reusable format.

Should you wish to complain about our response in any way this must initially be done by e-mailing [1][Hull City Council request email] or by contacting us at The Information Governance Team, The Guildhall, Alfred Gelder Street, Hull, HU1 2AA.

If you are not satisfied with the outcome of the internal review then you may take your complaint to the Information Commissioner's Office, the government body established to enforce the legislation.

Information Commissioner's Office

Wycliffe House Water Lane,

Wilmslow,

Cheshire,

SK9 5AF

So Hull City Council use as the excuse that there is not enough justification to release the information and the public interest in with holding the information outweighs the public interest in disclosure. Surely it is in the public interest that the public should know that Hull City Council along with other councils are mainly profiting out of the poorest in our society by way of highly inflating their summons costs. The council is unlawfully profiting out of summonsing people to the magistrates' court and claiming for costs that they have not reasonably incurred.

CHAPTER 7

NOTTINGHAM COUNCIL

My Ref:

Your Ref:

Contact:

Email:

Nottingham City Council

Resources – Strategic Finance
Loxley House
Station Street
Nottingham
NG2 3NG

Tel: 0115 8763649

Clerk to the Magistrates Court
Nottinghamshire Magistrates Court
Carrington Street
Nottingham
NG2 1EE

25 June 2015

Dear Sir or Madam,

Costs Application - Liability Orders

Regulations 34(5)(b) and 34(7)(b) of the Council Tax (Administration and Enforcement) Regulations 1992, provide for costs, reasonably occurred to be applied for and awarded to an Authority following issue of a summons and the granting of a Liability Order. A Schedule of Costs for a Liability Order application is set out below. It provides the Court with sufficient information to reach a proper judicial determination on whether the costs claimed represent costs reasonably incurred by the Authority in obtaining a Liability Order. The Schedule is provided having regard to the principles highlighted by the High Court in, R (Nicolson) v Tottenham Magistrates & London Borough of Haringey [2015] EWHC 1252.

The total costs per Liability Order application amounts to £70, with £50 incurred upon the issue of a summons and £20 upon the granting of a Liability Order.

Activity	Total FTE Hours	Total Hourly Rate	Cost Recharge £m	Cost per Summons £
Phone Calls	1,946	27.09	0.053	3.32
Letters & Emails	1,190	27.09	0.032	2.03
Counter Enquiries	550	27.09	0.015	0.94
Reminders Leading to Summons	**3,685**		**0.100**	**6.29**
Phone Calls	9,914	27.09	0.269	16.92
Letters & Emails	4,850	27.09	0.131	8.28
Counter Enquiries	1,120	27.09	0.030	1.91
Summons Administration	**15,885**		**0.430**	**27.11**
Court Officer			0.052	3.28
Staff Attending Court	219	27.09	0.006	0.37
Court Officer & Staff Attending Court	**219**		**0.058**	**3.65**

Contract IT Recharges	0.070	4.40
Contract Accomodation Recharges	0.155	9.74
Contract Receiving Payment Recharges	0.020	1.26
Contract HR Recharges	0.050	3.17
Contract Finance Recharges	0.055	3.49
Contract IAS19 Recharges	0.015	0.96
Contract Legal Recharges	0.072	4.56
Proportion of Recharges	0.438	27.58
Court Fees	0.078	4.91
Printing & Postage	0.023	1.43
TOTAL COST PER SUMMONS		70.98
TOTAL COST	1.127	
Summonses incurring costs	15,874	
TOTAL COST PER SUMMONS	70.98	

Notes	
Summonses incurring costs	15,874

Yours faithfully

Acting Head of Corporate Finance

NOTTINGHAM CITY COUNCIL SUMMONS & LIABILITY ORDER COSTS - DETAILED BREAKDOWN

STAFF COSTS	
TOTAL COUNCIL TAX SALARY COST 2014/15 INCLUDING ON COSTS	£2,000,000
SYSTEMS SUPPORT COSTS	£35,000
TOTAL FTE HOURS 2014/15	75,113
HOURLY COST	**£27.09**
SUMMONSES INCURRING COSTS AVG 2010/11 TO 2014/15	
ALL SUMMONSES ISSUED AVG 2010/11 TO 2014/15	26,000
SUMMONS CANCELLED PRIOR TO LIABILITY ORDER COURT AVG 2010/11 to 2014/15	3,635
SUMMONS CANCELLED POST COURT AVE 2010/11 to 2014/15	2,523
20% NON RECOVERY	3,968
RECOVERY SUMMONSES INCURRING COSTS	**15,874**
PROPORTION OF RECHARGES	
IT RECHARGES 2015/16	£265,000
ACCOMMODATION AND SUPPORT CHARGES 2015/16	£587,000
RECEIVING PAYMENT RECHARGE	£76,000
HR RECHARGES	£191,000
FINANCE RECHARGES	£210,000
BUSINESS SUPPORT RECHARGES	£58,000
PENSION RECHARGES	£275,000
LEGAL RECHARGES	£15,000
TOTAL STAFF HOURS ON RECHARGEABLE SUMMONS WORK	19,789
PROPORTION OF TOTAL COUNCIL TAX FTE HOURS FOR SUMMONS WORK	26.3%
REMINDERS LEADING TO SUMMONS	
ALL REMINDERS / FINALS ISSUED 2014/15	95,387
REMINDERS RESULTING IN SUMMONS	26,000
PROPORTION OF REMINDERS RESULTING IN SUMMONS	27.3%
TOTAL PHONE CALLS IN RESPONSE TO REMINDER	35,690
AVERAGE CALL AND WORK TIME (MINS)	12
TOTAL FTE HOURS ON PHONE CALLS FOR REMINDERS LEADING TO A SUMMONS	1,946
TOTAL LETTERS AND EMAILS IN RESPONSE TO REMINDER	17,482
AVERAGE WORK TIME (MINS)	15
TOTAL FTE HOURS ON LETTERS AND EMAILS FOR REMINDERS LEADING TO A SUMMONS	1,190
TOTAL COUNTER ENQUIRIES HANDLED FOR REMINDERS	4,033
AVERAGE HANDLING TIME (MINS)	30
TOTAL FTE HOURS ON COUNTER ENQUIRIES FOR REMINDERS LEADING TO A SUMMONS	550
TOTAL FTE HOURS	3,685
TOTAL HOURLY STAFF COST	£27.09
TOTAL COST RECHARGE	£99,843
RECOVERY SUMMONSES INCURRING COSTS	15,874
TOTAL COST RECHARGE PER SUMMONS	**£6.29**

SUMMONS ADMINISTRATION	
TOTAL PHONE CALLS IN RESPONSE TO SUMMONS	23,798
AVERAGE CALL AND WORK TIME (MINS)	25
TOTAL FTE HOURS ON PHONE CALLS FOR SUMMONSES	9,914
TOTAL LETTERS AND EMAILS IN RESPONSE TO A SUMMONS	11,641
AVERAGE WORK TIME (MINS)	25
TOTAL FTE HOURS ON LETTERS AND EMAILS FOR SUMMONSES	4,850
TOTAL COUNTER ENQUIRIES HANDLED FOR SUMMONSES	2,689
AVERAGE HANDLING TIME	25
TOTAL FTE HOURS ON COUNTER ENQUIRIES SUMMONSES	1,120
TOTAL FTE HOURS	15,885
TOTAL HOURLY STAFF COST	£27.09
TOTAL COST RECHARGE	£430,354
RECOVERY SUMMONSES INCURRING COSTS	15,874
TOTAL COST RECHARGE PER SUMMONS	£27.11
COURT OFFICER AND STAFF ATTENDING COURT	
ANNUAL SALARY INC ON COSTS OF COURT OFFICER	£40,000
CORPORATE MANAGEMENT OVERHEADS (30% of hourly staff cost)	£12,000
COST OF NON-RECOVERY	£0
COURT OFFICER COST	£52,000
FTE HOURS FOR STAFF ATTENDING COURT 2014/15	219
HOURLY STAFF COST	£27.09
STAFF COSTS	£5,933.24
TOTAL COST OF STAFF ATTENDING COURT	£57,933
RECOVERY SUMMONSES INCURRING COSTS	15,874
TOTAL COST RECHARGE PER SUMMONS	£3.65
PROPORTION OF RECHARGES	
IT RECHARGES	£69,815
ACCOMMODATION AND SUPPORT CHARGES	£154,648
RECEIVING PAYMENT RECHARGE	£20,023
HR RECHARGES	£50,320
FINANCE RECHARGES	£55,325
PENSION RECHARGES	£15,280
LEGAL RECHARGES	£72,450
TOTAL RECHARGES	£437,862
RECOVERY SUMMONSES INCURRING COSTS	15,874
TOTAL COST RECHARGE PER SUMMONS	£27.58
COURT FEES	
SUMMONS COURT FEES LEVIED	£78,001
RECOVERY SUMMONSES INCURRING COSTS	15,874
TOTAL COST RECHARGE PER SUMMONS	£4.91
PRINTING AND POSTAGE	
POSTAGE AND PRINTING COST PER REMINDER	£0.68
POSTAGE AND PRINTING COST PER SUMMONS	£0.75
TOTAL COST RECHARGE PER SUMMONS	£1.43
TOTAL COST RECHARGE PER SUMMONS	£70.98

CHAPTER 8

LAMBETH COUNCIL

HER MAJESTY'S COURTS SERVICE
hmcs

Mr M Hynes
Directorate of Legal & Democratic Services
London Borough of Lambeth
DX 132672 Brixton 2

19 January 2009

Deputy Justices' Clerk
Miss Thirza Mullins

Camberwell Green Magistrates' Court
15 D'Eynsford Road
Camberwell
London
SE5 7UP

DX 35305 Camberwell Green

T 020 7805 9801
F 020 7805 9895
E thirza.mullins@hmcourts-service.gsi.gov.uk

www.hmcourts-service.gov.uk
Our ref: TJM/nd
Your ref:

Dear Mr Hynes

Re: Level of Summons Costs for London Borough of Lambeth Council Tax Summonses

I write further to your letters of the 26th September and 29th December and our subsequent e-mail exchange concerning the increase in council tax summons costs for Lambeth.

The designated District Judge and Bench Chairman have now considered your claim to increase costs. They noted that your costs had not been increased since April 2006 and the calculations you had detailed reflecting increased costs to yourselves. They also however noted with concern that the increase was a significant inflationary one in the current economic climate.

In all the circumstances they have decided to agree to the increase in costs which may be claimed on each summons. However they would hope that the council will consider carefully the cases they bring to court in light of the current economic circumstances and be particularly sensitive to the financial circumstances of those households who have previously been good payers but may temporarily be experiencing financial difficulties.

I hope this information is of assistance and I apologise for the delay in the making of this decision.

Yours sincerely

T. Mullins

Miss Thirza Mullins
Deputy Justices' Clerk
Direct Line: 020 7805 9801
Email: thirza.mullins@hmcourts-service.gsi.gov.uk

Your ref:

Our ref:

26 September 2008

Lambeth
Legal Services

Chief Clerk
Camberwell Magistrates' Court
15 D'Eynsford Road
Camberwell Green
London
SE5 7UP

Level of summons costs for London borough of Lambeth Council Tax summonses

Dear Sir

As you will be aware, in previous years, the level of costs charged for Council Tax summonses and liability orders by London Boroughs were agreed centrally between the magistrates' courts and the London Revenues Group (LRG).

In May of this year, the notified all London Boroughs that they should agree these costs with their own individual magistrate court.

Therefore, I am writing to you to notify you that the London Borough of Lambeth will be raising the level of costs charged for their Council Tax summonses and liability orders from £90 and £5 to £122 and £5 respectively. This will result in the overall cost of recovery action for the non-payment of Council Tax to rise from £95 to £127.

I have attached a summary calculation showing how this level of costs has been reached. It should also be noted that part of the reason for this rise is due to the delay in the magistrates' central forum making a decision on the previous application from the LRG for an increase in the level of these costs. In fact these costs have not increased since April 2006.

For your information, I am aware that other London Boroughs have agreed the following levels with their courts

Barking & Dagenham £123
Harrow £130
Islington £125
Lewisham £125

London Borough of Lambeth
Legal Services
Lambeth Town Hall
London SW2 1RW
DX 132672 Brixton 2
Facsimile 020 7926 2361

And that other Boroughs are in the process of notifying their courts of their new levels.

I trust that the above fully explains the situation and I look forward to confirmation that Camberwell Magistrate's court will agree to this new level of costs.

Yours faithfully

Mark Hynes
Director of Legal & Democratic Services
Direct Line: 020 792 62209
Email: mhynes@lambeth.gov.uk

Enc

Calculation of Court Cost for 2008-09

Notices sent out during year

Type of notice	No.	%			Cost of Recovery
Initial bill	128,240	22%		CTAX Budget	£3,595,700.94
One off billing	230,552	40%		Ratio of recovery action	38%
Reminders	102,913	18%			
Finals	60,423	10%		Cost of Receovery	£1,360,929.91
Summonses	29,378	5%			
Liability Orders	25,783	4%		Magistrate court fee	3
				Estimate number of summonses issued	29,378
Total Notices	577,289	100%		Total estimate cost of magistrate fee	£88,134.00
Recovery Notices	218,497	38%			
				Total cost of recovery	£1,449,063.91

Cost of individual summons and LO cost

Type	No.	% actually charged	% in year collection	No of summonses collected against	Value of Costs to be charged	
Summons cost	29,378	65%	60%	11,457	£122.00	£1,397,805.24
LO cost	25,783	65%	60%	10,055	£5.00	£50,276.85
					£127.00	£1,448,082.09

LAMBETH SUBMISSION TO COURT 2008
Notices sent out during the year

Type of notice	No.	%	
Initial Bill	128,240	22.21	
One off billing	230,552	39.94	
Reminders	102,913	17.83	163,336
Final notices	60,423	10.47	
Summonses	29,378	5.09	
Liability Order	25,783	4.47	37.8488
Total Notices	577,289	100	
Recovery Notices	218,497		

Cost of individual summons and LO cost

Type	No.	% actually charged	% in year collection	No of summonses collected against
Summons cost	29,378	65%	60%	11,457
LO cost	25,783	65%	60%	10,055

= 39% collection rate

RECREATION OF COURT FIGURES from CIPFA return 2007/8
Notices sent out during the year

Type of notice	No.	%	
Initial Bill	127,227	22.66	
One off billing	223,711	39.85	
Reminders and finals	156,874	27.94	Only total figure available
		0.00	
Summonses	29,378	5.23	
Liability Order	24,203	4.31	37.4880
Total Notices	561,393	100	
Recovery Notices	210,455		

Cost of individual summons and LO cost CIPFA figures

Type	No.	% actually charged	% in year collection	No of summonses collected against
Summons cost	29,378	65%	60%	11,457
LO cost	24,203	65%	60%	9,439

65% x 60% = 39%. Collection rate wrong!

Reminders, paid before summons	127,496	0.2271	
Reminders to summons	29,378	0.0523	
Summonses	29,378	0.0523	
Liability Order	24,203	0.0431	0.1478
Total Notices	561,393	1	
Recovery Notices	82,959		

Cost of individual summons and LO cost (as approved)

Type	No.	% actually charged	% in year collection	No of summonses collected against
Summons cost	29,378		62%	18,214
LO cost	24,203		62%	15,006

Cost of individual summons and LO cost - reassessed to fit proper income

Type	No.	% actually charged	% in year collection	No of summonses collected against
Summons cost	29,378		62%	18,214
LO cost	24,203		62%	15,006

Cost of individual summons and LO cost   Using CIPFA collect

Type	No.	% actually charged	% in year collection	No of summonses collected against
Summons cost	29,378		70%	20,565
LO cost	24,203		70%	16,942

Cost of individual summons and LO cost REQUIRED to meet alleged costs   Using CIPFA collect

Type	No.
Summons cost	29,378
LO cost	24,203

CTAX Budget £	3,595,700.00	
Billing 62% £	2,229,334.00	2,229,334.00
No. of bills	358,792	
Cost of sending a bill	**£6.21**	
Reminder/Final Notice 28% £	1,006,796.00	1,006,796.00
No. of notices	163,336	
Cost of sending a reminder/final notice	**£6.16**	
Sumonses 5% £	179,785.00	179,785.00
No. of Summonses	29,378	
Cost of sending a summons	**£6.12**	
Liability Orders 4% £	143,828.00	143,828.00
No. of Liability Orders	25783	£77,349.00 Total cost of Liability
Admin cost of Liability Order	**£5.58**	
Magistrates' Court fee £	3.00	
Cost of obtaining/sending a Liability Order	**£8.58**	
		3,559,743.00

Cost of sending a summons £6.12

Lambeth Council are charging £122.00 for sending a summons.

Cost of Recovery
CTAX Budget   £3,595,700.94

Ratio of recovery action   38%

Cost of Recovery   £1,360,929.91

Magistrate court fee   3
Estimate no. of summonses issued   29,378
Total estimate of magistrate fee   £88,134.00

Total cost of recovery   £1,449,063.91

Value of costs to be charged

	£122.00	£1,397,805.24
	£5.00	£50,276.85
	£127.00	£1,448,082.09

Cost of Recovery
CTAX Budget   £3,595,700.94

Ratio of recovery action   37%

Cost of Recovery   £1,348,028.28

Magistrate court fee   3
Estimate no. of summonses issued   29,378
Total estimate of magistrate fee   £88,134.00

Total cost of recovery   £1,436,162.28

Value of costs to be charged

	£122.00	£1,397,805.24
	£5.00	£47,195.85
	£127.00	£1,445,001.09

and LO fee to LO
Cost of Recovery
CTAX Budget   £3,595,700.94

Ratio of recovery action   15%

CHAPTER 9

BARNET BOROUGH COUNCIL

PAUL PATTERSON made this Freedom of Information request to Barnet Borough Council.

https://www.whatdotheyknow.com/request/the_councils_costs_and_calculati#incoming-1412582

The council's costs and calculations approved by magistrates concerning summonses and liability orders.

8th June 2019
Dear Barnet Borough Council,
Will you please supply me with a copy of the councils costs and calculation which have been approved by magistrates for council tax summonses and liability orders 2018-19 and 2019-20, as I believe the Council has breached High Court Case ruling of: CO/976/2014

Rev Paul Nicholson v Tottenham Magistrates, because adding unreasonable costs to

the claim was unlawful.

Yours faithfully,

PAUL PATTERSON.

BARNET
LONDON BOROUGH

26 June 2019
Our ref: 5378028

Thank you for your request received on 8 June 2019, for the following information:

Dear Barnet Borough Council,
Will you please supply me with a copy of the councils costs and calculation which have been approved by magistrates for council tax summonses and liability orders 2018-19 and 2019-20, as I believe the Council has breached High Court Case ruling of: CO/976/2014 xxxxxxxxxxxx, because adding unreasonable costs to the claim was unlawful.

Yours faithfully,

We have processed this request under the Freedom of Information Act 2000.

Response

The council holds the information requested and the calculation is attached.

Dear Barnet Borough Council,
Will you please supply me with a copy of the councils costs and calculation which have been approved by magistrates for council tax summonses and liability orders 2018-19 and 2019-20, as I believe the Council has breached High Court Case ruling of: CO/976/2014

xxxxxxxxxxxxx, because adding unreasonable costs to the claim was unlawful.

When the Local Authority applies for Liability Orders, the calculation of our costs is provided to the bench at each hearing who decide if the costs are reasonable. As such, when the Magistrates grant the liability orders, they are approving our costs.

Further information

If you are interested in the data that the council holds you may wish to visit Open Barnet, the council's data portal. This brings together all our published datasets and other information of interest on one searchable database for anyone, anywhere to access.   http://open.barnet.gov.uk/

Advice and Assistance : Direct Marketing

If you are a company that intends to use the names and contact details of council officers (or other officers) provided in this response for direct marketing, you need to be registered with the Information Commissioner to process personal data for this

purpose. You must also check that the individual (whom you wish to contact for direct marketing purposes) is not registered with one of the Preference Services to prevent Direct Marketing. If they are you must adhere to this preference.

You must also ensure you comply with the Privacy Electronic and Communications Regulations (PECR). For more information follow this Link X X X X X

For the avoidance of doubt the provision of council (and other) officer names and contact details under FOI does not give consent to receive direct marketing via any media and expressly does not constitute a 'soft opt-in' under PECR.

Your rights

If you are unhappy with the way your request for information has been handled, you can request a review within the next 40 working days by writing to the Information Management Team at:XXXXXXXXXX. Or by post to Information Management Team (FOI) The London Borough of Barnet, North London Business Park, Oakleigh Road South, London, N11 1NP

If, having exhausted our review procedure, you remain dissatisfied with the handling of your request or complaint, you will have a right to appeal to the Information Commissioner at: The Information Commissioner's Office, Wycliffe House, Water Lane, Wilmslow, Cheshire, SK9 5AF (telephone: 0303 123 1113; There is no charge for making an appeal.

8th July 2019

Dear Kyrie Loizou,

You have not sent me the information that I asked for. I asked for a COPY of the councils costs and calculation for council tax summonses which have been approved by the magistrates 2018-2019 2019 - 2020

Yours faithfully,

Paul Patterson.

25th July 2019
Dear Mr Patterson

I have received the following response from the service in regard to your further request

We have provided our calculation and this is what is put before the Court at our liability order hearings.

We do not have an individual document that says the Court approve the costs we charge.

There is no standard format on how the calculation is made and the Magistrates on the day decide if they are satisfied or not with the application.

Thank you for your interest in Barnet Council.
Yours sincerely
Richard Carter
Information Management Officer
Assurance Group

2 Bristol Avenue, Colindale, NW9 4EW

29th July 2019
Dear Kyrie Loizou,
Barnet Council have not provided their costs and calculations. Anyone wishing to challenge their costs would need to see how the council calculated their costs, how they arrived at the said sum.
Rev Paul Nicoloson won his judicial review on the same grounds:
"iii) the Claimant was denied a fair opportunity to challenge the lawfulness of the order before it was made, by reason of the failure to answer his requests for the provision of information as to how the sum of £125 was arrived at."

http://www.bailii.org/cgi-bin/format.cgi?doc=%2Few%2Fcases%2FEWHC%2FAdmin%2F2015%2F1252.html&query=(Reverend)%20AND%20(Nicolson)&fbclid=IwAR3xJFy_XIp1FhZVQQiQS0knmq8pBgRmQlD6yzDJkM82cqBT2U38a3OV5aY

Yours sincerely,

PAUL PATTERSON

8th August 2019
Dear Mr Patterson

Thank you for your email.

My earlier response provided you with the Council's calculation and this is what is put before the Court at our liability order hearings.

There is no standard format on how the calculation is made and the Magistrates on the day decide if they are satisfied or not with the application.

There is no other information held that is in the scope of your request.

The Nicholson judgement to which you refer has been considered and our current practices are compliant with this. The Calculation of the reaonable costs in work involved in obtaining a Council Tax liability order is attached again for ease of reference.

Please do come back to me if you are seeking other information held by the Council.

Yours sincerely

**Richard Carter
Information Management Officer
Assurance Group**

2 Bristol Avenue, Colindale, NW9 4EW

Private and confidential - Commercial in confidence

Calculation of the reasonable costs in work involved in obtaining a Council Tax liability order

1. Barnet total gross cost of Council tax operation (2017/18) — £5,026,516.00 A

This amount includes all costs, direct staffing, staffing on-costs (pension and NI), support costs, accommodation, all relevant recharges (legal, finance, director, policy, committees etc), front and back office, computer costs, apportionment of debt charges

	Range of possible percentages	Appropriate percentage for particular authority		
1. General costs of operation in respect of customers that pay as due	5-25%	25%	£1,256,629.00	
2. Cost of dealing with customers that progress to reminder / final but do not progress to liability order	5-15%	10%	£502,651.60	
3. Cost of work post liability order	2-10%	10%	£502,651.60	
4. Cost of work involved in all activities in respect of those customers where it is necessary to make complaint and issue summons	45-65%	45% B	£2,261,932.20	£2,764,583.80
5. Cost of activities between summons and liability order hearing	2-10%	10% C	£502,651.60	
6. Total of percentages		100%		
6. Total numer of summonses issued		20119 D		
7. Total number of cases where liability order granted		15858 E		
8. Cost to be charged in respect of summons/complaint (A*B/D)		£112 F		
9. Cost to be charged in respect of liability order (A*C/E)		£32 G		
10. Total costs per case where case progesses to LO (F+G)		£144		

Barnet Borough Council's calculations of costs can be downloaded: -
https://drive.google.com/file/u/0/d/19ccPhGVoWFEX4V7s8WfCMft5-
JiZcLaJ/view?usp=sharing&pli=1

CHAPTER 10

ASHFORD BOROUGH COUNCIL

PAUL PATTERSON made this Freedom of Information request to Ashford Borough Council.
The council's breakdown of their costs and calculation concerning council tax.

https://www.whatdotheyknow.com/request/the_councils_breakdown_of_their#incoming-1429522

9th June 2019
Dear Ashford Borough Council,

Will you please supply me with a copy of the council's breakdown of their costs and calculations which have been approved by magistrates for council tax summonses and liability orders 2018-19 and 2019-2020

Yours faithfully,

PAUL PATTERSON.

10th July 2019
Dear Ashford Borough Council,
You have not replied to my FOI request the council's breakdown of their costs and calculation concerning council tax. Promptly, as normally required by law.

Yours faithfully,

PAUL PATTERSON.

Ashford Borough Council 12 July 2019

To determine the costs reasonably incurred in connection with the application it is not practical to calculate and provide a breakdown of costs for each application. Therefore, for standard cases, the costs incurred will be determined by calculating and aggregating the costs incurred in a previous period and dividing this figure by the number of summonses. Calculation of Costs 2018/19 Salaries, Postage, Communications, Computer Hardware, Computer Software, Legal &; Professional fees, Stationery &; printing, Mileage &; expenses, Service recharge Recovery Costs Recovery Costs Council Tax NDR £335,880.00 £44,831.00 £125.00 £180.00 Regarding the 2019/20 calculation I would advise that this is being reviewed therefore further information is not currently available.

If you are dissatisfied with the handling of your request, you have the right to ask for an internal review. Internal review requests should be submitted within two months of the date of receipt of the response to your original letter and should be addressed to: Tom Swain, Governance and Data Protection Officer, Ashford Borough Council, Civic Centre, Tannery Lane, Ashford, Kent TN23 1PL If you are not content with the outcome of the internal review, you have the right to apply directly to the Information Commissioner for a decision. The Information Commissioner can be contacted at: Information Commissioner's Office, Wycliffe House, Water Lane, Wilmslow, Cheshire, SK9 5AF Please remember to quote the reference number above in any future communications.

12th July 2019

Dear Ashford Borough Council,

I understood the breakdown of costs you have supplied, but you still have not given me a copy of that breakdown, how the council came to them figures. I want a copy of the working of those figures, they can not just be plucked out of thin air.

Yours faithfully,

PAUL PATTERSON.

9th August 2019

Dear Ashford Borough Council,

Will you please send me a copy of the council's aggregated costs that you have stated in the format presented to the magistrates for their approval.

Yours faithfully,

PAUL PATTERSON.

11th September 2019

Dear Sir To determine the costs reasonably incurred in connection with the application, as previously stated - it is not practical to calculate and provide a breakdown of costs for each application. Calculation of Costs 2018/19 includes Salaries, Postage, Communications, Computer Hardware, Computer Software, Legal &; Professional fees, Stationery &; printing, Mileage &; expenses &; Service recharges. Calculation of Costs Recovery

Costs Recovery Costs Ctax NNDR Salaries £151,740.00 £5,517.00 Office Equipment £300.00 £0.00 Postage (1st class / airmail / hand delivery costs) £10,370.00 £1,500.00 Mobile Phones £120.00 £0.00 Computer Hardware £150.00 £0.00 Computer Software £8,400.00 £5,100.00 Legal &; Professional Fees £28,600.00 £7,190.00 Recovery Notices stationery / printing £16,710.00 £900.00 Mileage &; expenses £1,596.00 £147.00 Shared Services £10,500.00 Contact centre / CSA / print room recharges £73,704.00 £1,806.00 IT Recharges / system jobs / reporting, complaint lists, court lists £16,962.00 £8,979.00 Central Admin Recharges £27,228.00 £3,192.00 £335,880.00 £44,831.00 If you are dissatisfied with the handling of your request, you have the right to ask for an internal review. Internal review requests should be submitted within two months of the date of receipt of the response to your original letter and should be addressed to: Tom Swain, Governance and Data Protection Officer, Ashford Borough Council,
Civic Centre, Tannery Lane, Ashford, Kent TN23 1PL If you are not content with the outcome of the internal review, you have the right to apply directly to the Information Commissioner for a decision. The Information Commissioner can be contacted at: Information Commissioner's Office, Wycliffe House, Water Lane, Wilmslow,

Cheshire, SK9 5AF Please remember to quote the reference number above in any future communications.

The first thing I noticed with Ashford Borough Council was that I never had the name of any person responding to my requests.

CONCLUSION

There are around 3.5 million summonses sent out by councils each year in England & Wales. People need to start attending their hearings, they need to insist on seeing the magistrates that they have been summonsed to stand before.

After entering the magistrates' court you will be approached by a council worker, not a court officer, and the council employee will try and get you into a side room and simply get you to agree to instalments, the council will then be granted a liability order against you. You have to refuse the council employees invite into the side room, insist that you be removed from their bulk listing, this you should have done when you sent your legal notice to the council and court.

By removing yourself from the bulk listing you are treated as an individual, and by doing so in mass, the court and councils will be thrown back to the way of the old poll tax where it was taking the magistrates 18 months to 2 years to hear each case.

*As of 7th September as I am ready to print this book, it has been brought to my attention that some councils are now starting to summons people to their council tax hearing. Nottingham City Council is sending out summonses, issued on 3rd September 2020 inviting people to mass gathering, this is unlawful.

Rochdale Council is sending out summonses, which Greater Manchester Magistrates' Court states on them that the hearings will be conducted by telephone. If this is the case, and the court and council are doing this to get round the covid-19 restrictions, every person summonsed should telephone the court and council stating they dispute the councils costs and ask for a breakdown of these cost so you can make a lawful challenge. Everyone must telephone the council and state they will be attending the magistrates' court. Remember the council summons 1,000 – 2,000 people to these hearing all on the same day and time.

This looks like Rochdale Council setting about inventing administrative processes, a 'SCAM' or a massive misapprehension by the authorities and the courts. A mistaken belief, about or interpretation of a statutory provision.

Good morning

I can confirm that such hearings can take place via telephone and I am aware that this is a process that is in place in Greater Manchester. I have copied in my counterpart who is responsible for this in Greater Manchester and I have no doubt he will be able to assist with any specifics relating to Rochdale.

I hope that helps

Regards

Janine Burke

Senior Legal Manager (Crime Business) North West Region

9th September 2020
Hi Janine,

Thank's for the speedy reply, but can you show me which regulation states that a liability order hearing for council tax can be conducted over the telephone. The council tax regs state 'to appear before the court'

Paul Patterson.

Hi

I believe it is contained in legislation that was recently passed - The Health Protection (Coronavirus) Regulations 2020.

However, I am not involved in the processes personally – I have copied in my colleague in GM who is involved.

Hope that helps

Janine Burke

Senior Legal Manager (Crime Business) North West Region.

Application for liability order
34.
(2) The application is to be instituted by making complaint to a justice of the peace, and requesting the issue of a summons directed to that person to appear before the court to show why he has not paid the sum which is outstanding.

Nothing stated in the regulation about a hearing by telephone, the regulation states 'to appear.'

https://www.legislation.gov.uk/uksi/1992/613/regulation/34/made
The councils fraud and deceit needs to be stopped, and if the magistrates and judges will not do it, the masses need to stand together and bring it all to a halt.

ENFORCEMENT AGENTS ENTERED THE WRONG PROPERTY FOR THE WRONG PERSON

On 12th April 2018 Gregg Binding & Stefan Wackett enforcement agents (EX COPPERS, THAMES VALLEY) unlawfully enter my home.

https://www.youtube.com/watch?v=D1OIKpBmjq0
https://www.youtube.com/watch?v=u9m8v3iMp38

They came to the wrong property for the wrong person. Binding thinking he could stop any court action handed in his licence to get back his £10,000 bond. When this failed he went to the High Court Royal Courts of Justice to appeal, he lost his appeal and Gregg Binding & Stefan Wackett were ordered to appear at Milton Keynes County Court. The hearing was to decide if they were both fit to be Enforcement Agents.

HHJ Rochford's judgement was that they were both fit person to be enforcement gents.

HHJ Rochford in his judgement stated that Binding should not be condemned for his actions but rather commended.

HHJ Rochford states that none of the video evidence shows Binding to be the aggressor. He stated, "They do demonstrate him using restraint techniques, notably a hold to the neck area, that most people might be reluctant to deploy, or would not know how to deploy."

"But Mr Binding is a former police officer, trained in such techniques."

This I have now found to be untrue, police officers are not taught to use neck restraints in the officers safety training programme.: -

https://www.met.police.uk/SysSiteAssets/foi-media/metropolitan-police/disclosure_2017/november_2017/information-right-unit---police-officer-training-to-apply-a-choke-hold-to-a-persons-neck-and-circumstance-when-this-would-be-justified

When Enforcement Agents attack you in your own home and the Police fail to attend...#pattersongate
https://www.youtube.com/watch?v=rxTQnLbSqOo

Throughout my case Hertford County Court have done nothing but made error after error. It started with:

1. Her Honour Judge Bloom dismissing my case because Binding had surrendered his licence before the hearing on 29th June 2018
I complained in writing to Judge Bloom that it was wrong to dismiss my case, she then agreed that she made an error.

2. The court did not put my complaint to Judge Bloom until some five months after they had received it.

3. The court allowed Binding to surrender his licence and recover his £10,000 bond without first checking he had no live complaints against him. High Court Judge Mr Pushpinder Saini stated in his judgement this was wrong. It was never explained how Binding surrendered his licence on 9th June 2018 which was a Saturday, a day the courts are closed.

4. His Honour Judge Rochford in my view has erred. He has not taken into consideration case law. He stated Binding should not be condemned, but commended for his 'bold' actions.

So His Honour Judge Rochford judges that both Binding & Wackett are fit persons to hold enforcement agents licence.

My next stage now is to go for a judicial review on points of law.

Binding v Patterson
[2019] EWHC 2665 (QB)

Queen's Bench Division

Pushpinder Saini J 15 October 2019

Judgment
Chris Royle (instructed by Feltons Law) for the Appellant
Paul Patterson (Litigant in Person) for the Respondent
Hearing date: 9 October 2019

- - - - - - - - - - - - - - - - - - - -

Approved Judgment
I direct that pursuant to CPR PD 39A para 6.1 no official shorthand note shall be taken of this Judgment and that copies of this version as handed down may be treated as authentic.

....

MR JUSTICE PUSHPINDER SAINI

MR JUSTICE PUSHPINDER SAINI :
This judgment is divided into 7 sections as follows:

- I. Overview: paras.1-7
- II. The Statutory Framework: paras. 8-11
- III. Facts and Procedural Chronology: paras. 12-28

- IV. Ground 1: paras. 29-43
- V. Ground 2: paras. 44-54
- VI. Ground 3: permission to appeal: paras. 55-58
- VII. Conclusion: para. 59

I. Overview

1. This is an appeal about the regulation of certificated enforcement agents (formerly known as "certificated bailiffs"). The appeal is brought by Gregg Ashley Binding ("Mr. Binding") against two Orders of HHJ Bloom ("the Judge") made on 14 February 2019 and 22 February 2019, respectively, in the Hertford County Court. The claim in which these orders were made was a complaint under Regulation 9 of the Certification of Enforcement Agents Regulations 2014 ("the CEA Regulations").

2. At the time the proceedings were commenced in the County Court, Mr. Binding was a certificated enforcement agent under section 64 of the Tribunals, Courts and Enforcement Act 2007. The proceedings concerned a complaint of serious misconduct made against Mr. Binding by the Respondent to the appeal, Mr. Paul Patterson ("Mr. Patterson").

3. I will return to the detail of the complaint below but, in brief outline, Mr. Patterson alleges he was assaulted by Mr. Binding when he sought entry to Mr. Patterson's personal residence in Looe on 12 April 2018. The allegations are contested by Mr. Binding.

4. Relying on his allegations above, Mr. Patterson says that Mr. Binding is not a "fit and proper person" (within the meaning of the CEA Regulations) to hold a certificate as an enforcement agent and sought to put that issue before the County Court under the procedures I set out below.

5. The main issue in this appeal does not concern the merits of the claims of misconduct but is a question of law concerning the scope and application of the CEA Regulations in circumstances where an enforcement agent has, before disposal of those proceedings, voluntarily surrendered his certificate to the County

Court. In short, Mr. Binding says that this act puts an end to proceedings while Mr. Patterson argues to the contrary.

6. As will appear below, the case has an unfortunate procedural history and with respect to the Judge there is no reasoned judgment from the Court below as to what the Judge's decision was on this core issue of law. One can infer however from the recitals to a number of orders made (without hearings) what the Judge considered the answer to be. It appears that originally the Judge decided that the proceedings were indeed at an end following surrender of the certificate, but she later reversed that decision and reinstated the proceedings with directions for a full trial of Mr. Patterson's complaint.

7. Aside from the main issue of law (which is Ground 1), there are further grounds of appeal (Ground 2) and an application for permission to raise a new ground of appeal (Ground 3) which concern the procedural propriety of the Judge's orders by which she reinstated the proceedings.

II. Statutory Framework

8. The role and intrusive powers of certificated enforcement agents demand a form of regulatory control over their conduct. Parliament has sought to achieve such control by creating a judicial forum for complaints to be made against such agents in the County Court. That has been achieved by way of the CEA Regulations (in addition to processes for ensuring only "fit and proper" persons are in the first instance authorised to act as such: see Regulations 3 and 4).

9. A number of provisions of the legislation are material to the appeal and I will set those out below in full because of the issues of construction which arise. The material parts of the CEA Regulations are as follows:

"9. Complaints as to fitness to hold a certificate

(1) This section has no associated Explanatory Memorandum

(1) Any person who considers that a certificated person is by reason of the certificated person's conduct in acting as an

enforcement agent, or for any other reason, not a fit person to hold a certificate, may submit a complaint in writing to the court.

(2) No fee is payable for submitting a complaint under paragraph (1).

(3) A complaint submitted under paragraph (1) must provide details of the matters complained of and explain the reason or reasons why the certificated person is not a fit person to hold a certificate.

(4) No complaint submitted under paragraph (1) may be considered by the judge until the certificated person has been provided with a copy of the complaint and given an opportunity to respond to it in writing.

(5) If on considering the complaint and the certificated person's response the judge is satisfied that the certificated person remains a fit and proper person to hold a certificate, the complaint must be dismissed.

(6) If—

(a) the certificated person fails to respond; or

(b) on considering the complaint and the certificated person's response the judge is not satisfied that the certificated person remains a fit and proper person to hold a certificate,

the complaint must be considered at a hearing.

(7) If a complaint is to be considered at a hearing under paragraph (6)—

(a) the certificated person must attend for examination and may make representations; and

(b) the complainant may attend and make representations, or may make representations in writing.

(8) If after a hearing the judge is satisfied that the certificated person remains a fit and proper person to hold a certificate, the complaint must be dismissed.

(9) No appeal lies against the dismissal of a complaint under paragraph (5) or paragraph (8).

10. Cancellation or suspension of certificates

This section has no associated Explanatory Memorandum

(1) If, following consideration of a complaint at a hearing, the judge is satisfied that the certificated person is not a fit and proper person to hold a certificate, the judge may—

(a) cancel the certificate; or

(b) suspend the certificate.

(2) If the certificate is cancelled, the judge may order that the certificated person must, before making any further application to be issued with a certificate, have fulfilled such conditions as to training or any other conditions as the judge considers necessary for the certificated person to be a fit and proper person to hold a certificate.

(3) If the certificate is suspended the judge may order that the suspension is not to be lifted until the certificated person has fulfilled such conditions as to training or any other conditions as the judge considers necessary for the certificated person to be a fit and proper person to hold a certificate.

(4) The court must, whether the certificate is suspended or cancelled, consider whether to make an order under regulation 13(2).

11. Application of security after consideration of complaint at a hearing

This section has no associated Explanatory Memorandum

(1) When a complaint has been considered at a hearing, the judge may, if satisfied that the complaint was well founded, order that the security be forfeited either wholly or in part, and that the forfeited amount be paid, in such proportions as the judge considers appropriate—

(a) to the complainant by way of compensation for failure in due performance of the certificated person's duties as an enforcement agent or for the complainant's costs or expenses in attending and making representations; and

(b) where costs or expenses have been incurred by the court in considering the complaint at a hearing, to Her Majesty's Paymaster General by way of reimbursement of those costs or expenses.

(2) The judge may make an order under paragraph (1) whether or not the certificate is cancelled or suspended.

(3) If an order is made under paragraph (1) but the certificate is not cancelled, regulation 6(4) applies.

(4) If the certificate is cancelled, the security must, subject to the making of an order under paragraph (1), be cancelled and the balance of any deposit, following payment of any amounts ordered to be forfeited, returned to the certificated person.

12. Surrender of certificate

This section has no associated Explanatory Memorandum

(1) When a certificate is cancelled or expires, it must be surrendered to the court, unless the judge directs otherwise.

(2) If a certificated person ceases to carry on business as an enforcement agent, the certificated person must unless the judge orders otherwise surrender the certificate to the court, and the certificate will be treated as if it had expired on the date on which it was surrendered.

(3) The security must be cancelled and the balance of any deposit returned to the certificated person following surrender of a certificate".

10. It is clear that under the procedural regime of Regulation 9, once a complaint has been submitted in accordance with the requirements of Regulation 9(3) (as was the case here) and (pursuant to Regulation 9(4)) the certificated person has been given an opportunity to respond there are only two forms of further order available to the Judge: (a) a form of summary dismissal on the basis that the written materials submitted satisfy the Judge the person remains a fit and proper person to hold a certificate (Regulation 9(5)); or (b) reference of the matter for an oral hearing if the certificated person has not responded or the Judge considers he is not satisfied the person remains a fit and proper person to hold a certificate.

11. The procedure for making complaints is provided for by CPR 84.20 which is in the following terms:

"84.20 Complaints as to fitness to hold a certificate

84.20-(1) This rule applies to a complaint under regulation 9(1) of the Certification Regulations.

(2) The complaint must be submitted to the County Court hearing centre at which the certificate was issued, using the relevant form prescribed in Practice Direction 4.

(3) A copy of the complaint must be sent to the applicant within at least 14 days before the hearing, and the applicant may respond both in writing and at the hearing.

(4) The complainant is not liable for any costs incurred by the certificated person in responding to the complaint, unless paragraph (5) applies.

(5) The court may order the complainant to pay such costs as it considers reasonable if it is satisfied that the claimant-

(a) discloses no reasonable grounds for considering that the certificated person is not a fit person to hold a certificate; and

(b) amounts to an abuse of the court's process."

III. <u>Facts and Procedural Chronology</u>

12. As indicated above, Mr. Patterson's allegations against Mr. Binding of misconduct are serious and disputed. In order to provide a broad flavour of what is alleged, I will refer to the witness statement of Mr. Patterson (provided to HHJ Bloom on 26 September 2018) which he states (in relevant respects) as follows:

"….I opened the door, there were two males all dressed in black, I later discovered they were called Gregg BINDING and Stefan WACKETT. Mr. Wackett who was stood behind Mr. Binding stated that they had a liability order for Jamie Patterson. I stated that no Jamie Patterson lives here. Mr. Binding said they were here to enforce a court order. At this point they were standing in my porch. I asked them several times to leave but they wouldn't. I told them to get outside and I would talk to them, but they refused. At this point I told my daughter to keep filming while I get them both out, I put my hands up to try to push them out. Before I made any contact with Mr. Binding, he pushed me backwards down onto the stairs. I got up and went into the kitchen adjacent to the stairs and called the police 999. Whilst I was talking to the police Mr. Binding started to go through a pile of letters on the windowsill in front of me. These were letters about my daughter's doctor's appointment. I grabbed the letters off Mr. Binding as he had no right to them. My daughter is vulnerable and epileptic. He then shouted out that I assaulted him, which I hadn't, at no time did I ever assault Mr. Binding. Mr. Binding while I was still talking to the police immediately kicked out at my stomach and grabbed me by the throat, Mr. Binding pushed me backwards a number of metres into the back passage leading to the back door of the house. I ended up against the passage wall with Mr. Binding still tightly holding me by the neck, I was struggling to breath and I was really frightened and fearing for my life, the pressure was so great I thought I was dying. As I was sliding down the wall Mr. Binding kept on saying "STOP RESISTING". I was not resisting at all I didn't have any strength. Mr. Binding not only stopped me from breathing, he put pressure on the blood vessels to my head. My daughter Toni had tried to fight Mr. Binding off me from the time he grabbed me by the throat, at no time did Mr. Wackett try to help Toni get Mr. Binding to realise his grip on my throat. Mr. Binding finally let go and I slumped into a seating position. Mr. Wackett then stated that we should all calm down and that he was recording it all".

13. Although it was not apparently before the Judge at the time of the original 5 July 2018 Order (referred to at paragraph [19] below), there was produced to me during the appeal a document entitled Enforcement Agent Report dated 8 May 2018 where Mr. Binding says in response (identifying the most material aspects):

-

"Upon attendance I read a notice in the front window regarding enforcement agents. This stated along the lines that any attendance would be charged at a certain amount per hour. We proceeded and knocked on the door. There was no reply and I noticed the door was not locked and therefore we entered peacefully, as per legislation. I then knocked on the inner door and just a few seconds later a male came to the door and asked us to hang on, which we did. I explained we were looking to speak to Jamie Patterson. Whilst inside of the premises waiting I noticed there were several court related papers pinned onto a notice board which seemed very strange to me. The door was then answered by a male who was immediately aggressive and was swearing at us. He had a small video recorder in his hand at this time. He stated that there was no Jamie Patterson living at the address. Under normal circumstances if the person answering the door had either simply engaged with us and told us that there was no such person at the address or had slammed the door then we would no doubt at all have just left the address and written up the notes to that effect and that would have been the end of the matter. Instead, the male handed the video recorder to a female called Toni and immediately assaulted me. He grabbed hold of me and pushed me backwards, so much so that my back hit the open outside doorway. I was forced to defend myself and had to push him backwards. I am totally satisfied that this is within the law as the male had already assaulted me. My actions were only because of his violence towards me and not only necessary but justified. Following this the male then went into the kitchen and rang the police, whilst I stood in the hallway. It is normal that if anybody does ring the police for any reason that the police will ask to the speak to the enforcement agent and I will always explain the reasons for my attendance. The police will expect me to do so".

-

14. There has been no judicial resolution as to whose account is accurate but it is fair to observe that the nature and type of allegations made by Mr. Patterson raised a serious case to answer as to Mr. Binding's fitness to remain entitled to a certificate. His Counsel rightly did not suggest to the contrary. This is clearly not a case which could have been summarily dismissed by the County

Court Judge under Regulation 9(5) on the basis of the merits of the written allegations and written response.

- 15. I will now turn to the rather confused procedural chronology which I have sought to piece together from the documents as supplemented with information requested by me of the parties during the hearing of the appeal.

- 16. On 24 April 2018, Mr. Patterson submitted a complaint ("the Complaint") concerning Mr. Binding's conduct to the County Court. It contained essentially the allegations I have summarised above.

- 17. There is no dispute that this was properly a complaint within the terms of Regulation 9(1) of the CEA Regulations. No response to the Complaint (as provided for by Regulation 9(4)) was in the appeal bundle before me but after making a request of the Appellant's representatives during the appeal the document (Enforcement Agent Report) to which I make reference above was helpfully produced to me in court. This may well be the document to which the Judge below made reference in the recitals to the Orders under appeal (see paragraph [25] below).

- 18. At some point after the submission of the Complaint on 24 April 2018 and before 29 June 2018, Mr. Binding voluntarily surrendered his certificate to the County Court (presumably under Regulation 12(2)). I have been able to identify from the Enforcement Report that his certificate was in fact not to expire for some time (12 August 2019). This was a very early surrender. I draw no conclusions from that but it is fair to observe that Mr. Patterson saw this as a deliberate tactic from Mr. Binding to avoid the Complaint going forward.

- 19. On 29 June 2018, at a sitting of the County Court at Hertford, HHJ Bloom dismissed the Complaint. It is common ground that this Order was made without any application by Mr. Binding, without a hearing and without any notice to the parties. The Order recording that dismissal (itself dated 5 July 2018- the date I will use below to refer to this Order) stated that this dismissal was "Upon Mr. Binding having surrendered his certificate and the certificate thefore [sic] being treated as having expired on 9th June 2018".

20. There are no further reasons before me as to the basis for HHJ Bloom's Order of 5 July 2018 but it appears clear from the recital that she decided to dismiss the complaint not on the merits but solely because Mr. Binding had surrendered his certificate.

21. In my view, and as will be clear from my comments on the statutory framework above, this was not a determination under Regulation 9(5), namely a judicial decision that the complaint fell to be dismissed because the Judge was satisfied Mr. Binding remained a fit and proper person to hold a certificate. It was a dismissal which was not on any legal basis one can find in the CEA Regulations. Doing the best I can, it seems that the Judge decided that it was implicit in the regime of the CEA Regulations that surrender of a certificate (provided for by Regulation 12) would put an end to extant proceedings concerning the fitness of an enforcement officer. I will return to this matter when I consider Ground 1 below.

22. Mr. Patterson told me at the hearing of the appeal that he received the 5 July 2018 Order of HHJ Bloom shortly after it was made and sought legal advice. He is a person of limited means. He also said he was unwell at this time. There was a substantial delay of over 2 months before he took any relevant action.

23. That action was on 26 September 2018 when Mr. Patterson (acting in person) applied to have the Order of 5 July 2018 (in his words) "quashed" on the basis that Mr. Binding was not a fit and proper person and complaining that by reason of the dismissal of his complaint "there is no redress". Mr. Patterson provided a witness statement supporting this application. It is not clear in the Application Notice what jurisdiction Mr. Patterson was asking the Judge to exercise in "quashing" the 5 July Order. He also asked for the application to be dealt with without hearing. His Application Notice identified the correct address for service on Mr. Binding but it regrettably appears that Mr. Binding did not receive the application (it being the responsibility of the County Court to send it to him). Nothing then happened for about 5 months. That was not Mr. Patterson's fault.

24. On 14 February 2019, HHJ Bloom set aside her Order of 5 July 2018 as requested by Mr. Patterson in his application and made various directions for the hearing of the substantive complaint together with the complaint made by Mr. Patterson against Mr. Wackett. Again, there was no hearing before this Order was made

(no hearing having been requested by Mr. Patterson) and the delay in the making of this Order is explained on the face of the Order of 14 February 2019. It was because, regrettably, Mr. Patterson's application had not been put before HHJ Bloom until 28 January 2019.

- 25. It is to be noted that the Judge recorded in a recital to the Order of 14 February 2019 that Mr Binding had filed a response to the complaint and she expressly said "...the complaint must proceed pursuant to Regulation 9(6). This appears to be a determination not to dismiss the Complaint and to proceed to a hearing (the second of the options I refer to in paragraph [10] above). The Judge also expressly provided in paragraph 9 of the 19 February 2019 Order for a liberty for either party to apply within 7 days of service to have the Order set aside. That is important for reasons to which I will return under proposed Ground 3.

- 26. For reasons which are not clear, HHJ Bloom varied the Order of 14 January 2019 by a further Order dated 22 February 2019 which specifically recorded in the recital as follows: "...Upon the court considering the complaint and the response and the judge not being satisfied the certificated person remains a fit and proper person to hold a certificate and that there must be a hearing to resolve the complaint under Regulation 9". The Judge clearly had in mind here the terms of Regulation 9(5) and wanted to make it apparent she was making a formal determination insofar as the earlier order had not made that clear. The balance of the procedural directions in the 22 February 2019 remained essentially the same as those in the 14 January 2018 Order (including the liberty to apply to set aside).

- 27. No application to set aside was made by Mr. Binding. Instead, he appealed to the High Court. On 3 April 2019, Thornton J refused permission to appeal (on the papers) against the 14 and 22 February 2019 Orders of HHJ Bloom. Lang J granted permission to appeal following an oral renewal on 7 May 2019.

- 28. I am informed that the Appellant did not receive the Application Notice and witness statement of Mr. Patterson (which led to the making of the 14 and 22 February 2019 Orders) until after Lang J had granted permission to appeal. That matter is relevant to the application to pursue a new ground of appeal (proposed Ground 3).

IV. Ground 1

29. It was persuasively argued by Counsel on behalf of Mr. Binding that there was no jurisdiction to proceed with a complaint against him because a complaint under the CEA Regulations may be brought only against a certificated person. Counsel accepted that at the date of the complaint Mr. Binding was a certificated person but it was argued that because he was permitted to surrender his certificate, having ceased to carry on his business as an enforcement agent, the definition of 'certificated person' necessarily implies that person continues to hold a valid and unexpired certificate. It was argued that the effect of surrender of a certificate upon ceasing to carry on business as an enforcement agent is to treat the certificate as having expired on the date of surrender (Regulation 12(2)) with the result that the previously certificated person's certificate is no longer valid and unexpired and he is thereby no longer a 'certificated person' and there is no jurisdiction under Regulation 9 to proceed with a hearing.

30. In support of this submission it was argued that the remedies (in cases where the respondent is not fit and proper) under the CEA Regulations are not capable of being granted or would be of no effect where a certificate has expired or been surrendered. Those remedies are cancellation or suspension of the certificate: Regulation 10(1), and/or forfeiture of security: Regulation 11(1). Security is returned to the previously certificated person on expiry or surrender of the certificate: Regulation 12(3). Thus, it is argued, there is nothing to cancel, suspend or forfeit. Further, it is said that those remedies apply only to a 'certificated person', which Mr. Binding was not (at the time of these grounds), and will not be at the time of any hearing.

31. So, the essential argument made on Mr. Binding's behalf was that (irrespective of the wisdom of such a legislative choice- a matter to which I return below), the net effect of the provisions of the CEA Regulations to which I have made reference above was that once a person had surrendered his certificate a complaint under Regulation 9 had to be dismissed. The logic of this submission is to my mind that the expiry of a certificate also leads to this consequence.

32. Counsel argues that the original dismissal of the Complaint by HHJ Bloom by the Order of 5 July 2018 was correct in law and the reinstatement of the proceedings by the Orders of 14 and 22 February 2019 was wrong in law because surrendering the certificate ended the ability of the Court to continue with hearing the Complaint.

33. It was rightly and realistically accepted by Mr. Binding's Counsel that this might be a highly undesirable outcome given the public interest (which one sees at play in other professional regulatory contexts) in not allowing persons to escape regulatory scrutiny by resigning or retiring from regulated roles. I should add that there is no evidential basis for suggesting in this case that this is why Mr. Binding surrendered his certificate but on his arguments it will be a result of such action that the events of 12 April 2018 in Mr. Patterson's house in Looe will never be subject to judicial scrutiny under the CEA Regulations.

34. In my judgment, there is a simple answer to the Appellant's arguments under Ground 1:

(i) Regulation 9 allows a complaint to be made about a "certificated person's conduct". A certificated person is defined as "a person to whom a certificate has been issued".

(ii) The Appellant was (at the time the Complaint was issued on 24 April 2018) a person to whom a certificate has been issued.

(iii) That fact establishes the jurisdiction of the County Court over him for Regulation 9 purposes.

(iv) In order for the County Court to lose jurisdiction, there would need to be some express or implied wording in the CEA Regulations which requires a complaint to be dismissed on the surrender or expiration of a certificate.

(v) It is common ground that there is no express wording so providing.

(vi) Equally, I see nothing in the CEA Regulations which would justify the submission that Parliament had impliedly provided that complaints must be dismissed when a certificated person ceases to be certificated.

-

(vii) Indeed, for reasons given above, it would be contrary to the public interest and effective regulation for an agent to be able to avoid judicial consideration of his conduct by simply surrendering a certificate (or indeed through the happenstance of his certificate expiring in the period between a complaint being made any disposal of the complaint under Regulation 9). Certificates last for 2 years under Regulation 7.

-

35. In my judgment, HHJ Bloom's Order of 5 July 2018 was wrong in law and (subject to the further Grounds of Appeal) there was a basis in law under the CEA Regulations to continue to proceedings notwithstanding the surrender of the certificate by Mr. Binding.

-

36. I should add that the draftsman could easily have made express provision for such a disposal on surrender but it seems to me that for good reasons no such provision was made. Even if a person is no longer certificated (which can happen for reasons including simple expiry or surrender), there are strong public interest reasons why an independent and impartial judicial authority such as the County Court should be able to determine whether, while the certificate was extant, the conduct of the person holding it was such as rendered them no longer fit and proper to hold it.

-

37. I need also to address the argument made on behalf of Mr. Binding that the regime of sanctions identified in Regulations 10 and 11 apply only to those who at the date of the hearing hold a certificate. That may be so but there is nothing in the CEA Regulations to say that proceedings have to conclude with one of these sanctions. I do not read Regulation 10(1) (which is permissive in specifying the sanctions of cancellation or suspension of a certificate) as denying a court to give a judgment on a complaint where the certificate has expired. A court could simply make a declaration or findings of misconduct. This point is reinforced when one sees that the power of the Court to make financial remedies under Regulation 11(2) can be used whether or not cancellation or suspension is ordered.

-

38. In short, I do not see anything in the sanctions or remedial regime which impliedly requires an end to the complaints process on either surrender or expiration of a certificate.

39. As identified above, a further argument was made for Mr. Binding by reference to Regulation 12 which essentially provides a regime for surrender of a certificate (on the person ceasing to act as an enforcement officer or on cancellation/expiry of a certificate) with the consequences that the security of £10,000.00 (see Regulation 6(4)) is returned to the former certificated person. It was said that if Regulation 9 proceedings could continue against a person who had surrendered a certificate the "pot" of security which might be the subject of the only possible financial remedy under Regulation 11 would have been paid away before the proceedings would end.

40. I consider this point has a simple answer. The payment back of security is expressly subject to the court's power not to allow surrender of a certificate (see Regulations 12(1) and 12(2)) and in an appropriate case a court could refuse to allow surrender if Regulation 9 proceedings were extant and it wished to ensure the retention of security pending those proceedings. That was not done in this case and I assume the security has been paid back but I do not read the terms of Regulation 12 as standing in the way of determination of the Complaint even if security has now been paid back to Mr. Binding.

41. The facts of the present case suggest that it would be good practice in future for any County Court which is dealing with expired, cancelled or surrendered certificates under Regulation 12 to ensure that there are no outstanding Regulation 9 complaints against the relevant agent and (if there are) to ensure that the security remains intact pending final resolution.

42. Finally, I should record that it was argued before me that the public interest is protected even if proceedings come to an end on surrender. It is said that if a person applies for a new certificate (having originally surrendered a certificate when facing Regulation 9 proceedings) the Court will have on file the unresolved complaint and will be able to take it into account when considering a new application. I accept that Counsel for the Appellant has substantial experience in this area of the law and that this may well be the practice. That practice does not seem to me however to provide an

attractive or reassuring answer. First, there is no legislative obligation I have seen requiring a County Court to keep on file such unresolved matters. Second, the new application may come many years after the unresolved complaint and it is difficult to see how a court could easily resolve what may be a historic dispute.

43. For all these reasons I reject Ground 1 and hold that a CEA Regulation 9 complaint can be heard by the County Court even if a person has surrendered his certificate or it has expired. The Judge was right to reconsider her original order and to reinstate the proceedings (subject to the further procedural complaint which I will now address).

V. Ground 2

44. The argument under this ground is that there was no jurisdiction to re-open the question of dismissal of the complaint as the Judge did by way of her Orders of 4 and 22 February 2019 following Mr. Patterson's application of 26 September 2019. It was submitted on behalf of Mr. Binding that in law there was no jurisdiction in the County Court to list the Complaint for a hearing having previously dismissed the Complaint on paper.

45. It is said that this order was a final order. Reliance is placed on Kaminski v Martin [2018] EWHC 3800 (QB). It is further argued that the Orders amounted to allowing an appeal against the Court's own order and/or without jurisdiction because the overall effect of the Orders that the Judge set aside or varied her order of 5 July 2018 without hearing further argument and without any change in circumstances or other grounds to do so. To change a final order in those circumstances amounted, it is argued, to allowing an appeal against the Judge's own earlier Order (or to do that which can only be done by way of appeal). That is said to be wrong in law because (i) the Court has no power to allow an appeal against itself and/or (ii) in any event no such appeal lies by virtue of reg. 9 of the 2014 Regulations.

46. In my view, these arguments miss their target. As I have indicated above, I do not consider the Order of 5 July 2019 was in fact or in law a Regulation 9(5) dismissal on the merits. It was in fact an order which the Judge had no power to make for the reasons I have given above.

47. Further, unlike the position before Soole J in the Kaminski case, there was no lawful Regulation 9(5) dismissal and it is obvious for the reasons given by Soole J why such a dismissal cannot be reopened consistently with the regime under Regulation 9. That is not this case. The Kaminski case is not on point.

48. Further, I do not consider the Order of 5 July 2019 to be subject to the very tight restrictions on reopening final orders identified in the case law under CPR 3.1.(7).

49. In my view, the Order of 5 July 2019 was (on the evidence before me) made by the Judge of her own motion and without notice to the parties. It accordingly fell within CPR r.3.3. The Order made none of the provisions informing Mr. Patterson he could apply to set it aside. It is worth setting out CPR r.3.3 in full to emphasise how it requires important safeguards for those who are subject to the order including an ability to ask the court to reconsider. It provides

"Court's power to make order of its own initiative

3.3—(1) Except where a rule or some other enactment provides otherwise, the court may exercise its powers on an application or of its own initiative.

(Part 23 sets out the procedure for making an application)

(2) Where the court proposes to make an order of its own initiative—

(a) it may give any person likely to be affected by the order an opportunity to make representations; and

(b) where it does so it must specify the time by and the manner in which the representations must be made.

(3) Where the court proposes—

(a) to make an order of its own initiative; and

(b) to hold a hearing to decide whether to make the order,

it must give each party likely to be affected by the order at least 3 days' notice of the hearing.

(4) The court may make an order of its own initiative without hearing the parties or giving them an opportunity to make representations.

(5) Where the court has made an order under paragraph (4)—

(a) a party affected by the order may apply to have it set aside, varied or stayed; and

(b) the order must contain a statement of the right to make such an application.

(6) An application under paragraph (5)(a) must be made—

(a) within such period as may be specified by the court; or

(b) if the court does not specify a period, not more than 7 days after the date on which the order was served on the party making the application."

50. There is nothing in the CEA Regulations or CPR which disapplies CPR 3.3. None of these CPR 3.3 safeguards and rights were identified in the 5 July 2018 Order. The Judge had power to reconsider the original order having heard representations from Mr. Patterson.

51. Further, in my judgment, the setting aside was not a process which was subject to CPR r 3.1 (7) and the strict limitations on reopening final orders (see Terry v BCS Corporate Acceptances Limited [2018] EWCA Civ 2422 at para. 68 and following). Asking the court to reconsider an order which it made of its own initiative and without any representations having been made does not require an applicant to show any change of circumstances. The process is governed by CPR 3.3.

52. There was admittedly delay in the period 5 July 2018 and 26 September 2018 in Mr. Patterson making the application to set aside

(or in his words to "quash" the 5 July Order), but in fairness to him he had not been informed (as he should have been on the face of the order) of his ability to apply to set aside the 5 July 2018 Order, and it would have been manifestly unfair to hold him to time limits which apply to those who have been so informed. I also accept that he needed some time to obtain legal advice and was unwell in this intervening period.

53. I accordingly reject Ground 2. There was clearly a jurisdictional basis for HHJ Bloom to reconsider her original Order of 5 July 2018. I should record that the existence of such a jurisdiction does not depend on the Judge or a party expressly identifying that jurisdiction on the face of an order in an application. Jurisdiction exists or it does not: it cannot be created or said not to be present merely by reason of what is said in an order or application notice.

54. Before leaving this ground and standing back from the unfortunate procedural history I have set out above, it hardly seems consistent with basic principles of fairness or the overriding objective for any party (let alone a litigant in person) to be precluded from asking a judge to reconsider her decision when that decision was made: (a) on the court's own initiative and without any application, evidence or argument; (b) without any notice that it was to be made; and (c) without any information being provided to the litigant that he had a right to set it aside. There is clearly an important interest in an application to set aside such an order being made as soon as practicable but on the facts before me, the delay by Mr. Patterson was justifiable and caused little prejudice in itself to the Appellant.

VI. Ground 3: permission to appeal

55. Under this proposed new ground of appeal the Appellant wishes to complain that he had no notice of Mr. Patterson's application of 26 September 2018 (indeed, he did not even have a copy until after permission to appeal was granted). He also wishes to complain that the application was dealt with without a hearing.

56. Permission to amend is required: CPR r.52.17. The test for amendment of an appeal notice is set out in Clarke v Lightning & Lamps (UK) Ltd [2016] EWCA (Civ) 5, per Vos LJ at [32]-[35]. I accept that the amendment was intimated well in advance of the

appeal hearing and there is good reason for it being made after the original grounds were filed (the relevant documents only having been received after Lang J's grant of permission to appeal). However, I do not accept this new ground has real prospects of success (having in fact heard full argument on it).

57. My reasons for refusing permission to appeal for this reason can be shortly stated as follows. First, the application which is attacked was not made by Mr. Patterson on a without notice basis. He correctly identified the name and address of the Appellant and it was not through any fault of Mr. Patterson that the Court failed to properly serve Mr. Binding. Second, I do not regard there as being anything wrong in principle with Mr. Patterson indicating (and the court accepting) that his application should be dealt with on paper. Third, this was not an appeal against the Judge's own earlier decision: it was an application in substance that she reconsider that decision and there was jurisdiction so to do for the reasons I have given above. Fourth, and most importantly, HHJ Bloom expressly and fairly provided the ability to Mr. Binding to apply to set aside her orders of 14 and 22 February 2019. That dealt with any unfairness in the process as a matter of case management. The procedural unfairness complained of could have been ventilated before the Judge under this liberty to apply.

58. There was no arguable error. This was an appropriate case management decision which fairly dealt with the situation which was presented to the Court and provided a mechanism for reconsideration. I refuse permission to amend to include the proposed new ground of appeal.

VIII. Conclusion
IX.

59. The appeal is dismissed. The Complaint against Mr. Binding should now be listed for directions and trial as soon as practicable and to be heard together with the existing complaint against Mr. Wackett. It would be regrettable for there to be further delay.

In the	
COUNTY COURT AT HERTFORD	
Complainant	Mr Paul Patterson
Enforcement Agent	Stefan Wackett and Gregg Binding

General Form of Judgment or Order

Paul Douglas Patterson
2 Tremayne Terrace
Widegates
Looe
Cornwall PL13 1QW

Before His Honour Judge Rochford sitting at Milton Keynes on 12th March 2020.

Upon the hearing of complaints by Mr Patterson against Mr Binding and Mr Wackett

Upon hearing oral evidence on 17th January 2020 and receiving written submissions thereafter

IT IS ORDERED THAT

The complaints be dismissed with no order for costs

IN THE HERTFORD COUNTY COURT SITTING AT MILTON KEYNES
[No Court reference number]

IN THE MATTER OF THE CERTIFICATION OF ENFORCEMENT AGENTS REGULATIONS 2014

AND IN THE MATTER OF A COMPLAINT UNDER REG 9 THEREOF
AGAINST MR GREGG BINDING

AND IN THE MATTER OF A COMPLAINT UNDER REG 9 THEREOF
AGAINST MR STEFAN WACKETT

Judgment delivered 12th March 2020

His Honour Judge Rochford:

I direct that pursuant to CPR PD 39A para 6.1 no tape recording shall be taken of this Judgment and that copies of this version as handed down may be treated as authentic

REASONS AND DECISION

Introduction
- These are my reasons and decision upon the hearing of a complaint brought by Mr Paul Patterson against Mr Greg Binding and a complaint brought by Mr Patterson against Mr Stefan Wackett. Both complaints arise from an incident that occurred on 12th April 2018 and have therefore been heard together. The complaints are made under regulation 9 of the Certification of Enforcement Agents Regulations 2014 (SI 421 of 2014) ("CEAR").

- I heard evidence in respect of the complaints at a one day hearing on 17th January 2020. I heard oral evidence from Mr Patterson, from his daughter Miss Toni Patterson, and from Mr Binding and Mr Wackett. Some time was taken in the viewing of various videos of the incident that is central to this complaint. Mr Patterson presented his complaint in person, and had the assistance of a McKenzie friend, Mr Docherty. Mr Binding and Mr Wackett were represented by Mr Royle (Counsel). I have received written closing submissions from Mr Patterson and on behalf of the Respondents. I have also received a "Response to the Closing Submissions for the Respondent" from Mr Patterson dated 09/02/20 (although in fact emailed on 13th February)("the Complainant's Response"). Mr Patterson gave evidence by reference to his two complaints and a document headed "Second Witness Statement of Paul Patterson".

- Mr Binding was permitted by me to provide his address in writing only, on a sheet of paper retained on the Court file. He indicated that service of any legal proceedings upon him before 17th January 2022 could be effected by serving him at the office of his solicitors Feltons Law, at 48 High Street, Cranbrook, Kent TN17 3EE (or wherever they may be in practice at the time). The solicitors' representative at Court indicated their agreement to this. I record that fact in this judgment in case any proceedings do in the future, but before that date, need to be served upon Mr Binding and there is any difficulty about it; Mr Patterson would be entitled to draw this paragraph to the Court's attention if the situation were to arise where he needed to make an application for substituted service or for service to be dispensed with.

- Although Mr Patterson had posted a copy of the "Second Witness Statement of Paul Patterson" to the respondents' solicitor, it had apparently not been received before the hearing. In the event, the hearing was able to proceed, and who (if anybody) was at fault for the non-receipt is not relevant to my decision. Subsequently, with his closing submissions (but not required by me), Mr Patterson has sent to the Court the Post Office's "Track and Trace" documents that show that the Post Office tried to deliver an item (doubtless this) to the Respondent's solicitor on 19th December 2019 (a Thursday), but there was nobody at the office. The time on the document (12.16pm) is the time at which it was available back at the Post Office. In his Complainant's Response, Mr Patterson returns to the subject, although it is not addressed in the Respondents' Closing Submissions and so is not a matter which ought to be addressed in such a response. Mr Patterson there suggests that the Post Office had left a card on 19th December; although the leaving of such a card might be normal practice, there is no evidence before the Court as to whether that was or was not done, nor was the assertion made in Mr Patterson' closing submissions. Mr Patterson states in the Complainant's Response that he believes this (ie the failure to collect the delivery) was a planned tactic by Feltons (the respondents' solicitors). These are issues that I need not resolve as I allowed Mr Patterson to rely on his statement and the exhibits, and Mr Patterson has suffered no conceivable prejudice or disadvantage by the alleged non-receipt by Feltons, and the Respondents take no point upon it. If anybody was disadvantaged, it was the respondents and their advisers.

- Miss Patterson gave evidence by reference to a statement.

- By his Complainant's Response Mr Patterson raises the issue of there having been contact between me and Mr Royle. He does not say what he suggests I should do about this. For the avoidance of doubt, I record here the position.

Recusal / bias
- At the outset of the hearing, I told Mr Patterson that I had had some contact with Mr Royle.

- The position is as follows:

  - I had previously dealt on paper with, and dismissed, an application by Mr Binding to dismiss the complaint without a full hearing.

  - In the course of dealing with that, I had noticed that the Court file contained a paper or lecture handout by Mr Royle on Certificated Enforcement Agents and complaints against them. It was a general paper, not specific to this case. I had not appreciated at that stage that Mr Royle was involved in this case. The reading of the Court file that it was necessary for me to carry out to deal with that application did not extend to a reading of the judgment of Pushpinder Saini

J (referred to below) or to anything else (the paper apart) that mentioned Mr Royle.

- I had assumed that the paper had found its way onto the Court file in the way that such papers can, especially where areas of law that are not routinely or frequently before the Courts are concerned. This is such an area. Such papers are not infrequently circulated within the legal profession and can be a valuable resource.

- I was aware that this case was likely to be listed before me. I was sitting away from the court where the Court file was located, but wanted to have access to Mr Royle's paper so as to enable me to familiarise myself with this area of the law before the case.

- I knew Mr Royle in a professional capacity. He had been a pupil barrister and, briefly after that, a practising barrister in the Chambers where I had practised. He had left those Chambers some years ago. It was a large set of Chambers. Our relationship was purely professional. So far as I can recall, I had had no contact with him since he left those Chambers.

- I therefore contacted him by email to his clerk asking for a copy of the paper. At no stage did I speak to him on the telephone and nor (contrary to what Mr Patterson says in his "Complainants Response") did I state that I had done this. Contact was initiated by me, for the purpose stated above. My initial email was to Mr Royle's clerk. I had found his clerk's email address through the internet, and had no other contact details for Mr Royle.

- I had no reason to and did not mention the name of the case to Mr Royle or his clerk. I was not aware that Mr Royle was involved in the case until the morning of the hearing.

- Mr Royle responded to my email. He sent me a copy of the paper. We exchanged a few emails; "professional pleasantries" is an accurate description of their nature. Emails were to and from my judicial email address.

- I explained the position to Mr Patterson at the outset of the hearing. He did not raise any concerns, or ask for time to consider the matter. He was content to proceed.

- I have again reviewed the position to consider whether I should have recused myself, or should now recuse myself. I have re-read the notes at para 1.1.2 in the White Book (Civil Procedure 2019). I note that there is no allegation of actual bias. Any recusal would be on the basis of apparent bias. I have asked myself whether the circumstances "would lead a fair-minded and informed observer to conclude that there was a real possibility or a real danger, the two being the same, that the tribunal was biased." Such a hypothetical observer would be aware of the fact that the nature of the legal profession is that there is often professional and, indeed, social contact between solicitors, barristers and judges. It is far from unusual for barristers to appear before judges who were in the same Chambers as them. Barristers and solicitors can often appear before judges with whom they may have quite close personal and social links. Such a hypothetical observer would not have regarded my request for the paper as unusual or untoward, and would have noted that I had raised the matter at the outset in a way that would have allayed any possible realistic concerns. I did not and do not consider recusal is necessary or appropriate.

- I note that Mr Patterson does not expressly seek my recusal, and does not suggest any course that he wishes me to take in respect of this contact, beyond seeking details in respect of it. I explained the nature of the contact at the start of the hearing, and have set it out above. No further disclosure is needed.

Background

- The complaints were commenced by Mr Patterson lodging forms at the County Court. He did this on 25th April 2018 in respect of 2018 Mr Binding and on 27th July 2018 in respect of Mr Wackett. Those are the dates stamped upon them by the Court office, indicating when they were received. Both complaints were submitted on forms referring to rule 8 of the Distress of Rent Rules 1988. CPR 84.20 requires the use of the from specified in CPR Practice Direction 4. The current form, and that which should have been used, is EAC 2, but nothing turns on the use of an incorrect or out of date form and, having regard to the overriding objective, I disregard the fact that an incorrect form has been used. Mr Patterson attached to each form a short statement setting out what he said took place.

- As at 12th April 2018 Mr Binding and Mr Wackett both held certificates issued by the County Court under s.64 of the Tribunals Courts and Enforcement Act 2007 ("TCEA 2007"). Mr Binding's certificate had been issued on 11th August 2017 and was due to expire on 10th August 2019. Mr Wackett's was issued on 1st February 2018 and was due to expire on 31st January 2020. I shall use the expression CEA, short for certificated enforcement agent, to refer to an individual to whom a certificate has been issued under s.64 of TCEA 2007. On 12th April 2018 they both worked in that capacity for Newlyn plc.

- At some point after the submission of the complaint against him, but before 29th June 2018, Mr Binding voluntarily surrendered his certificate to the Court, presumably under Regulation 12(2) of CEAR. I am told and accept that the £10,000 bond has been cancelled and any deposit returned, as required by Regulation 12(3) of CEAR. Pushpinder Saini J considered the effect of that surrender on these proceedings in a reserved judgment dated 15th October 2019 (Neutral Citation Number [2019] EWHC 2665 (QB)) and has determined that it does not bring an end to the complaint. Mr Royle has submitted to me that my powers in respect of Mr Binding, in the event that the complaint is upheld, are somewhat restricted; he submits that I cannot cancel or suspend Mr Binding's certificate under Regulation 10 of CEAR, as it has been surrendered, and nor can I order forfeiture of the security, it having been cancelled.

- Pushpinder Saini J set out aspects of the statutory framework under which certificated enforcement agents operate at paragraphs 8 to 11 of his judgment referred to above. I do not repeat what he said there, save for expressly noting and reiterating his observation that "[the] role and intrusive powers of certificated enforcement agents demand a form of regulatory control over their conduct."

- Regulation 3 of CEAR provides as follows:

    3. A certificate may be issued under section 64 of the Act only—

    (a) on application by the person to whom the certificate is to be issued; and

(b)if the judge is satisfied that—

(i)the applicant is a fit and proper person to hold a certificate;

(ii)the applicant possesses sufficient knowledge of the law and procedure relating to powers of enforcement by taking control of goods and of commercial rent arrears recovery to be competent to exercise those powers;

(iii)the forms which the applicant intends to use when exercising powers of taking control of goods or commercial rent arrears recovery conform to the design and layout prescribed in the Schedule to these Regulations;

(iv)the applicant has lodged the security required by regulation 6(1), or such security is already subsisting; and

(v)the applicant does not carry on, and is not and will not be employed in, a business which includes buying debts.

There are therefore five matter on which the Court must be satisfied before it can issue a certificate.

- In contrast, paragraphs (5) and (8) of Regulation 9 of CEAR 2014, which deal with the decision to be made on hearing of a complaint, both state

    "If …… the judge is satisfied that the certificated person remains a fit and proper person to hold a certificate, the complaint must be dismissed".

    So the extent of enquiry in the course of considering a complaint is more limited than on deciding whether to grant a certificate.

- The standard of proof is to the civil standard (balance of probabilities).

- Reg 9(7) of CEAR provides that on the hearing of a complaint the complaint "may" attend. In contrast, the certificated person "must attend for examination and may make representations." No sanction for non-attendance by the certificated person is laid down.

- In my judgment, the use of the word "remains" in Regulations 9(5) and (8) creates a neutral burden of proof. It reflects the fact that fitness will already have been established on the grant of the certificate. It also reflects the fact that the process on complaint is to an extent inquisitorial; it proceeds, even if the complainant does not attend. If there was a positive legal burden of proof upon the agent it is doubtful if CEAR would require his or her attendance for cross examination, even allowing for the fact that one could envisage a situation, absent this provision, of an agent not attending, but being represented and seeking to prove that they remained fit and proper by the calling evidence from others.

- Further, reg 10(1) of CEAR provides as follows:

    "10.—(1) If, following consideration of a complaint at a hearing, the judge is satisfied that the certificated person is not a fit and proper person to hold a certificate, the judge may—
    (a)cancel the certificate; or
    (b)suspend the certificate."

- If one reads either reg 9 or reg 10 as imposing a positive burden on the complainant or the certificated agent, there would be an obvious tension between the regulations. This further emphasises that the burden of proof is neutral.

- That the burden is neutral is common ground between the parties.

- I turn then to consider the enforcement mechanisms in respect of Council Tax.

- Regulation 34 of the Council Tax (Administration and Enforcement) Regulations 1992 (SI 613 of 1992) ("the CT Regs") provides for the making of a liability order by the Magistrates Court upon application by the council (authority) if Council Tax is unpaid. It appears from reg 34(6) that the court has no power to refuse an order if the conditions for the making of such an order are met.

- Reg 45 of the CT Regulations allows for distress to be levied where there is a liability order in force. It provides as follows:

  ### 45. Enforcement by taking control of goods
  Where a liability order has been made, payment may be enforced by using the Schedule 12 procedure.

  This is the version in force from 6th April 2014, the date on which Schedule 12 came into effect. In his closing submissions (at point 3 on page 8) Mr Patterson refers to para 45(5) of the CT Regulations, but he refers to the wording in force prior to 6th April 2014. The earlier version of Reg 45 allowed for the levying of distress where a liability order had been made and reg 45(5) provided as follows in those circumstances:

  (5) The person levying distress on behalf of an authority shall carry with him the written authorisation of the authority, which he shall show to the debtor if so requested; and he shall hand to the debtor or leave at the premises where the distress is levied a copy of this regulation and Schedule 5 and a memorandum setting out the appropriate amount, and shall hand to the debtor a copy of any close or walking possession agreement entered into.

- Mr Patterson's position is that a liability order granted by the magistrates' court gives no particular power to a CEA, and that Mr Binding and Mr Wackett had powers only as ordinary individuals seeking to collect a debt. That certainly appeared to be what he thought when he telephoned the police during the incident on 12th April 2018; he can be clearly heard on the video recording telling the police that that is the position. It appears to be his position that the issue of a liability order is some sort of administrative action akin to a demand sent by a person claiming to be owed money to the alleged debtor requesting payment

- Although he does not address the issue in his closing submissions, he does in his Complainant's Response.

    - He refers to and relies upon Reg 35(3) of the CT Regulations. He quotes from Reg 35(3) which states that "it [a liability order] is not to be treated as a sum adjudged to be paid by order of the court" ..... That is a somewhat selective quotation from Reg 35(3). In full it states:

(3) The amount in respect of which a liability order is made is enforceable in accordance with this Part; and accordingly for the purposes of any of the provisions of Part III of the Magistrates' Courts Act 1980 (satisfaction and enforcement) it is not to be treated as a sum adjudged to be paid by order of the court.

The effect of Part VI of the CT Regulations (Part VI extending from Reg 32 to Reg 57) is to create a code or mechanism for enforcement of liability orders.

- He refers also to an unidentified decision by a District Judge at the Middlesbrough County Court, where the Court seems to have accepted an apology in respect of a supposed "warrant of entry". I can deduce nothing from that decision, and do not consider it necessary or proportionate to seek further details from Mr Patterson about a decision that appears fact specific.

The position advanced by Mr Patterson is wrong; it is clear that legislation resulted in their powers as CEA's being engaged.

- A CEA has power to enter premises. This is a power granted by para 14 of Sched 12 to CEA 2007, which provides as follows.

14(1) An enforcement agent may enter relevant premises to search for and take control of goods.
(2) Where there are different relevant premises this paragraph authorises entry to each of them.
(3) This paragraph authorises repeated entry to the same premises, subject to any restriction in regulations.
(4) If the enforcement agent is acting under section 72(1) (CRAR), the only relevant premises are the demised premises.
....
(6) Otherwise premises are relevant if the enforcement agent reasonably believes that they are the place, or one of the places, where the debtor—
(a) usually lives, or
(b) carries on a trade or business.

- Note that:

  - There is no general power granted by the statute to use force to effect an entry. This is clear from para 17 of Schedule 12 which provides as follows:

    "17. Where paragraph 18, 18A, 19 or 19A applies, an enforcement agent may if necessary use reasonable force to enter premises or to do anything for which the entry is authorised."

    Where the paragraphs there listed do not apply, the statute does not provide a power to use force.

  - The power to enter must, in my judgment, include or imply a power to remain.

  - S.65 of TCEA 2007 provides and makes clear that Schedule 12 replaces the old common law rules. In the Complainant's Response, Mr Patterson suggests, by reference in particular to s.65(2), that the extent of this abolitions is limited. That submission ignores the clear and wide terms of s.65(1) and the fact that s.65(2) states that "The rules replaced include …". The list that follows is not an exhaustive list and does not limit that which is abolished.

- The power to enter premises is statutory. The fact that it does not include a power to use force to enter premises is a limit upon it. But the statutory power of entry does not depend upon permission being given by the occupier or owner. It derives from statute. So an owner or occupier cannot restrict the power by purporting to withdraw permission or forbid entry.

- Although there is an express power to "search for and take control of goods" that does not, on the face of it, include a power to search otherwise than to search for goods to take control of. Mr Royle submits that, because para 14 of Schedule 12 provides a test of reasonable belief, there must be some power granted to the CEA to test or verify his or belief. I reject that submission for the following reasons;

    - Para 14 relates to the definition of "relevant premises", and not of goods liable to be taken

    - Para 10 of Schedule 12 deals with the goods that may be taken, and provides as follows:

        "10 An enforcement agent may take control of goods only if they are goods of the debtor."

        There is no power to take control of goods that are not the debtors merely because the CEA harbours a reasonable belief that they are the debtors.

    - Mr Royle relies upon the case of *Rooftops South West Limited & others v Ash Interiors (UK) Limited & others* [2018] EWHC 2799 (QB) as persuasive authority to support his submission. He refers in particular to para 39 of that judgment. I do not read that paragraph, or any other part of the judgment of Master Davison, as having the effect contended for.

    - If Parliament had intended to provide CEA's with either an investigatory power (eg to look through documents with a view to gleaning information) or a more specific power to use documents to lead to the identification of goods of the debtor or to verify or otherwise a belief in ownership or property, it would have said so.

Events of 12th April 2018, and factual background

- The Complainant, Mr Patterson, lives at 2 Tremayne Terrace in Looe, Cornwall. Living with him is his daughter, Toni Patterson. She is over 18. Also living there, at least at the relevant time, was his 13 year old son. He remained upstairs during the event of 12th April 2018 apparently, and unsurprisingly, in a state of some distress.

- Mr Patterson's complaints are based upon what occurred on 12th April 2018. He is not required to set out or particularise how he puts any case in the manner of a pleading. In any event, given the inquisitorial nature of the hearing, the Court would not be bound or restricted by any such particularisation. But subject to that, Mr Patterson's complaints against the two men can, broadly, be summarised as follows:

    Mr Binding

    - Unlawful entry to the property
    - Violence when in the property

- Unlawful search through paperwork in the property
- Failing to wait for the police, instead driving off at speed.

Mr Wackett

- Unlawful entry to the property
- Failing to intervene in and stop Mr Binding's wrong-doing

Although not identified by Mr Patterson as an allegation against Mr Wackett, I will consider whether there was any wrongdoing on his part in failing to wait for the police, and (if this occurred) in driving off or being driven off at speed.

- I will also consider whether the evidence has raised issues about fitness that are not encapsulated in the above list.

- Mr Patterson has a long-standing and deeply held objection to paying council tax. It appears to be based on, or at least supported by, a belief that his local council spends or invests its money in an immoral support of the arms trade. His views on council tax are evidenced by posts on social media. He has written and self-published at least one book on the subject. Page 99 of the Respondent's bundle contains an image with the covers of two books he has written; they are either different books or different editions of the same book. The covers feature an image of military missiles of some sort.

- At exhibit 32 of his statement Mr Patterson has produced in evidence a notice that he displayed at his property. It is prominently headed "Door knockers please note". It states "This household charges £50 per minute to listen to sales pitches, religious messages, and fund raising stories. It charges £100 per minute to television "enforcement officers" (due to you being told time and time again that I do not watch a television) and bailiffs whether it be looking for me, or for someone who lived here previously. You will be filmed." I do not here reproduce the different typefaces etc used within that. The notice then sets out the contractual mechanism by which he, or his household, seeks to enforce such charges. The notice identifies various categories of individuals who are exempt from such charges, including "legitimate law enforcement officers , friends and family." The notice concludes, in block capitals, "ANY AND ALL IMPLIED RIGHTS OF ACCESS HAVE BEEN REMOVED". I deduce from that notice and its style that Mr Patterson takes a more antagonistic attitude than most people to the low-level annoyance caused by events such as unwanted callers.

- At around 6.30am on 12th April 2018 Mr Binding and Mr Wackett went to Mr Patterson's home. They went in their capacity as CEA's, and at the direction of Newlyn plc.

- The reason why they went was to collect money owed by a man called Jamie Patterson to London Borough of Haringey. Haringey LB had obtained a liability order from the magistrates court against Jamie Patterson in respect of his liability. Newlyn were of the opinion that Jamie Patterson lived at 2 Tremayne Terrace. He does not. Based on the evidence that I have, it appears that he is wholly unconnected to the complainant, Mr Paul Patterson. I do not know what had originally caused Newlyn plc to think that Jamie Patterson lived at that address.

- Two Notices of Enforcement had been sent by Newlyn plc to Jamie Patterson at 2 Tremayne Terrace. They are dated 12th February 2018 and appear (albeit in slightly cropped form) at page 100 of the Respondents' bundle. One can see a part of the name "Newlyn" on the notices there, and the name Newlyn was prominent on them. They appear there as part of a post made by the complainant to his Facebook page on 15th February 2018. He posted the following message with the images of the Notices of Enforcement (Respondent's bundle, p100)

    "Looks like I'll be having some fun with Newlyn in the next couple of weeks. Had couple of notices other week stating a J. Patterson owes L B of Haringey for CT. Now received notices stating name of Jamie Patterson, no one here of that name. When they see all the council tax info in my porch it may be hard to get them to believe a Jamie doesn't live here".

    The post concludes with two emojis; they appear to be laughing.

- It is clear from the sentence in that post that reads "Looks like I'll be having some fun with Newlyn in the next couple of weeks" that the complainant was expecting a visit from enforcement officers, or at least anticipated that there might be such a visit. It came a little later than the "couple of weeks" he referred to, but he was expecting or anticipating it. The precise meaning of, and inference to be drawn from, "having some fun" was the subject of cross examination.

- What happened when and after the two CEA's arrived at the house has been recorded on video, with audio recording. There are three recordings in all. One (in three parts) is from Mr Binding's body worn video, one from Mr Wackett's body work video and one from a "Go Pro" camera that Miss Patterson used, at the request or suggestion of her father. Mr Royle suggested he had that camera ready to film a confrontation. Mr Patterson said that the Go Pro was on his bicycle, just inside the house, and so just happened to be conveniently to hand.

- I have viewed the videos.

- I have also viewed a video that was posted on the internet.

- Mr Binding gave evidence to the effect that he had two liability orders against Jamie Patterson. In addition, he told me that he had access to Newlyn plc's records which indicated a recent payment had been made by Jamie Patterson, or in respect of his account. This, in his view, would give support to the belief that the address that Newly plc had for him was correct. He referred to the address as having been "cleaned" on the Newlyn data system. The details of this process were not explored, but they indicated a process of checking and ensuring that the necessary formal steps of giving notice had been taken before their attendance.

- Mr Binding took the lead in what occurred on 12th April 2018. That was the evidence of all concerned, and is plain from the videos. The Respondents' evidence to me, which I accept, was that Mr Wackett was comparatively new to his role, and was working with Mr Binding that day to gain experience or learn from him. He was receiving mentoring from Mr Binding. But Mr Wackett's experience was such that he was to take the lead in other visits and, of course, he was someone to whom a certificate had been issued by the Court.

- Mr Patterson adduced evidence to indicate that the two men were friends, with a strong personal relationship. Neither man disputed that.

- I find that when the men attended at Mr Patterson's property they both believed that there was a liability order outstanding against Jamie Patterson. That was correct. In addition, they believed that he lived at 2 Tremayne Terrace. That belief was not correct, but it was, in my judgment, one that they both held reasonably. In the case of Mr Wackett, his belief came predominantly from what he had understood from Mr Binding, but I do not consider that he acted unreasonably in so relying upon his colleague.

- Mr Patterson's evidence was that the men, or at least one of them (Binding) purported, before entering the premises, to be Jamie Patterson; he said words to the effect that it was Jamie. If that occurred, it would raise serious issues as to Mr Binding's conduct and fitness.

- This is not recorded on any of the videos. On the contrary, those record somebody (clearly Mr Binding) saying "Jamie, can we speak to him please". At this point, the CEA's are in the porch. They had been able to enter the porch because the outer door was not locked. The inner door was then, after some delay, opened by Mr Patterson. The delay is understandable, given the early hour. He responds by saying "Fucking Jamie what the fuck you on about". He then says no Jamie lives here. The two men then introduce themselves by name, saying they are from Newlyn plc.

- Whatever interpretation one places on "having some fun with Newlyn" Mr Patterson was, I repeat, expecting a visit from someone acting on Newlyn's behalf looking to collect money owed by a man called Jamie Patterson.

- Mr Patterson then telephoned the police. He says that the men are not bailiffs but are private debt collectors. In similar vein, Mr Patterson, having been told that the men have a liability order issued by the courts, takes issue with this. He maintains that a liability order is not a court order, but is a notice or statement. Mr Patterson then says that they are debt collectors not court bailiffs. He bases this on an apparent and expressed belief that CEA's have no role in council tax collection. He was aware that the men were CEA's; they had introduced themselves as such, and Mr Wackett was wearing his certificate prominently on a lanyard around his neck. On a number of occasions during the events that follow Mr Patterson can be heard telling Mr Binding that he (Mr Binding) has lost his job. Plainly, this is because Mr Patterson regards him as acting improperly. A factor in that was undoubtedly Mr Patterson's view that CEA's had no role or authority in the collection of Council Tax.

- I do not consider it necessary to attempt a line by line analysis of each section of the video evidence, or to try to compare it with the oral evidence of the witnesses.

- The evidence of the two respondents is that the outer door was open. Mr Patterson did not disagree with this. It is clear that they effected an entry without force into the porch. That was a lawful entry. They then spoke to Mr Patterson through the closed inner door, which was in due course opened to them.

- There was then an altercation around the inner threshold. In the course of that Mr Binding's body worn camera became dislodged by 180 degrees; it can be seen that a section of the footage is upside down.

- But at some point both men entered the inner part of the property through the open inner door, with no physical resistance.

- In my judgment, having regard to what one can see of the structure of the porch, which seems to be quite substantial and an integral part of the living accommodation of the property, the porch is part of the property, and the men effected an entry to the premises by entering that porch. If I am wrong, the subsequent entry through the inner door was not an entry by force and was therefore lawful.

- There are a number of physical altercations between Mr Binding and Mr Patterson. Mr Patterson alleges that during one of these, which took place in the kitchen, he was the victim of a karate kick by Mr Binding. He also said that Mr Binding subjected him to a knee in the stomach. I wanted to make sure that I understood precisely what Mr Patterson meant by a karate kick, especially when juxtaposed with the evidence of a knee to the stomach. Accordingly, I asked Mr Patterson to demonstrate during his evidence what he meant. Despite his years, Mr Patterson presents as a slim and fit man. He demonstrated a kick with the leg out straight and the toe pointed, and the leg raised to or above the horizontal. Indeed, even allowing for the fact that Mr Binding is taller that Mr Patterson, a kick to the stomach would have to involve the leg being raised above the horizontal, there being no suggestion that Mr Binding was raised up, for example on a step, or Mr Patterson crouching down. Such was the nature of the kick demonstrated in Court by Mr Patterson that I was momentarily concerned lest he might lose his balance in Court as he demonstrated it.

- No such kick can be seen recorded by any of the three cameras. The space in the kitchen is somewhat confined. The evidence of Mr Binding and Mr Wackett was that there was no such kick.

- I bear in mind the medical evidence (ie the medical records), and the account given by Mr Patterson, both on the phone to the police and to medical staff.

- Balancing all the evidence, I find that Mr Patterson, and his daughter, are wrong in saying that there was a karate kick. There was no such kick. Likewise, there was no knee to the stomach.

- It was suggested that Mr Binding deliberately turned his body worn camera off so that it would not capture his inappropriate behaviour. His explanation for his video recording being in three sections is this. He says that the camera rotated on his person. Because of its design, when it was upside down, he mistakenly thought it was turned off. In trying to turn it on, he in fact turned it off. I have already referred to the fact that the footage shows it did turn through 180 degrees. Neither the footage from Mr Wackett's body worn camera, nor from Mr Patterson's Go Pro, demonstrate a marked change in what I might call "tempo" or atmosphere when Mr Binding's camera is turned off. I reject the suggestion that he deliberately turned the camera off to enable him to act improperly during a period when the video was not recording

- What the evidence, notably the video evidence, demonstrates is that there were a number of physical altercations between Mr Binding and Mr Patterson. They do not demonstrate Mr Binding to be the aggressor in any of them. They do demonstrate him using restraint techniques, notably a hold to the neck area, that most people might be reluctant to deploy, or would not know how to deploy. But Mr Binding is a former police officer, trained in such techniques. Mr Patterson referred to his airway being restricted and to his having been rendered unconscious or nearly so. He places reliance on medical records which I have seen. Whilst I can and do readily accept that the restraint techniques used on Mr Patterson are likely to have been uncomfortable and distressing for him, the evidence does not suggest that he was unconscious or close to that. In my judgment, the techniques were properly used by a former police officer. I reach that finding despite the absence of evidence about the details of Mr Binding's training, or when he last had training, and bearing in mind that he had left the police service before these events.

- Mr Binding and Mr Wackett could have withdrawn at an early stage from the property. But there was no legal obligation on them to do so. I am satisfied that Mr Binding felt that he was there lawfully. He was correct in that view. He also felt that he could best discharge his duties by remaining on the premises. No doubt the easiest course for him would have been simply to withdraw at the first hint of any difficulty. He is not to be condemned, and, indeed, is to be commended, for taking a rather bolder course.

- The difficulty arose in part because Mr Patterson wrongly believed that the men had no lawful right to be there. He regarded them simply as private debt collectors, who he was entitled to eject, by force if needs be. He was wrong about that.

- Where and to the extent that there were physical altercations between Mr Binding and Mr Patterson, I am satisfied that these occurred because Mr Patterson acted as the aggressor.

- The question being whether Mr Binding remains a fit and proper person, fine questions as to the law of self-defence do not necessarily fall to be determined. That said, I am satisfied that what Mr Binding did amounted to no more than lawful self-defence. But in any event, he was responding to a fast-moving situation. To the extent that he was guilty of any misjudgement as to, for example, the degree of force necessary (and I do not consider that he was) those misjudgements would not render him other than fit and proper.

- After Mr Binding and Mr Wackett left the property, a measure of calm descended. The video demonstrates a calm and measured conversation at a nearby bus-stop between Mr Patterson and Mr Binding, in the course of which Mr Patterson shows Mr Binding a poster on the bus-stop, apparently about his book. Mr Binding had spoken to the police. Mr Binding and Mr Wackett drove off in the same vehicle. In my judgment, they were not trying to escape detection or avoid the police. They say they drove off in a normal manner. I do not conclude that there was anything unreasonable in their choosing to go, or in the manner of their going.

Three particular issues

- There are three aspects in respect of Mr Binding's behaviour that require specific and further consideration. The first is the fact that he did not show any paperwork to Mr Patterson. The second is the circumstances in which he came to have possession of, and retained possession of, the Go Pro. The third is his examination of paperwork in the house.

- Towards the start of the incident Mr Patterson can be heard to say "Show us your court order, court order". No order is shown at that stage, or, indeed, at any later stage. That request to be shown a court order is made after there has been a degree of violence or physical altercation. One of the CEA's tells him it is a liability order. At that point the atmosphere is tense but reasonably calm. Mr Patterson says "I know you were going to say that." He goes on to say that he has been getting letters for Jamie Patterson for about ten years. Mr Patterson is heard to tell his daughter to keep the video running, and directs her to step backwards, clearly better to capture the scene, saying something to the effect that "this is going to be smashing." Events rapidly move on from that request to see the court order. The stance of Mr Patterson, which he can be heard stating on the telephone to the police, is that, in respect of Council Tax, they have only the powers of private debt collectors. At one point he explains to the police on the telephone that he is an expert in Council Tax. The request to see any court order is not repeated. There is then a further physical altercation.

- I have asked myself whether Mr Binding (or Mr Wackett) ought to have shown a copy of the liability order at that point to Mr Patterson. In the light of Mr Patterson's very clear view that a liability order was not a determination or order of the Court, it is unlikely that it would have made any difference. But that is a view expressed by me with the benefit of hindsight, and does not assist me in determining the issue in this complaint, which requires me to judge the actions of Mr Binding and Mr Wackett based on what they knew or ought to have known at the time. The answer to the question as to whether any order or authorisation ought to have been shown at the time of that request or after lies in how events developed. The request was not, at least so far as the video and other evidence shows, repeated subsequently. Events rapidly escalated and overtook any request. I would not criticise either of the respondents for not, either at that stage or later, producing any paperwork. I would certainly not regard it as indicating that either of them was not a fit and proper person to hold a certificate. Although, as noted above and relied on by Mr Patterson, there was previously an obligation under reg 45(5) of the CT Regulations to carry and produce on request the authorisation of the local authority, that is no longer the case and, further, this referred to the authorisation and not to the Court order, and no request was made for that authorisation.

- Mr Binding was unable to explain precisely how the Go Pro came into his possession. That part of the incident can be seen on Mr Wackett's video. Mr Binding's account was essentially that the Go Pro ended up in his hand during a scuffle. Mr Patterson said that Mr Binding took the Go Pro outside. He is undoubtedly correct in that. He also says that Mr Binding was fiddling with the Go Pro as if trying to delete what it had recorded. What can clearly be heard on the video is Mr Binding saying words to the effect that he would seize the Go Pro for the police. The police had by that stage been called and the expectation was that they would attend. It would make little sense for him to want to destroy the footage on the Go Pro. Both his and Mr Wackett's body worn cameras recorded, and he would have expected them to have recorded, most of the incident in a reasonably clear way (allowing for the circumstances). There was no reason to suppose that the Go Pro would contain anything significantly different. Had he deleted the Go Pro footage this could be said in itself to have been suspicious. And had he stolen or otherwise retained or disposed of the Go Pro camera as a whole that would likewise have caused suspicion to fall on him, as well as, justifiably, exposing him to serious allegations. I do not consider that his actions in respect of the Go Pro reflect poorly on him or would lend any support for a finding that he was not a fit and proper person. I accept his evidence that he did not attempt to delete the footage on the Go Pro. As the video shows, he returned the Go Pro to Mr Patterson reasonably promptly once the situation became calm.

- I have indicated above my view that, as a matter of law, a CEA does not have power to search through paperwork looking for information. But the law in this area is not clear cut or straightforward. Indeed, the entire law about the powers and responsibilities of a CEA is complicated. The paperwork was out in a pile in the kitchen. Mr Binding picked it up and did begin to look through it. Whilst it can be said that Mr Binding should not have looked at the paperwork, even though it was openly out in the kitchen (and not, for example hidden away in a drawer), I do not regard his actions as any more than a minor misjudgement in a difficult situation. It was regrettable that the papers included, according to the evidence I have heard and which I accept, medical paperwork relating to Miss Patterson. I bear in mind the sensitivity that is, rightly, nowadays attached to confidential information in an age when digital access means that such information can readily be misused and transmitted. It was not suggested that Mr Binding was looking through paperwork other than to find out about Jamie Patterson, and whether he lived there (which was Mr Binding's evidence). Accordingly, I do not consider that that action renders him unfit.

Social media posts – Mr Patterson

- I turn back to Mr Patterson's post of 15th February 2018 and his assertion there that he would be "having some fun with Newlyn in the next couple of weeks." The respondents suggest that he was expecting some form of contact and confrontation (not necessarily physical) with Newlyn, and was, indeed, relishing the prospect. This would be consistent with his attitude to council tax and, by extension, collection of it. It is also consistent with the fact that he had made no attempt to contact Newlyn to explain that he had no connection with Jamie Patterson, which would have been the reaction of somebody who had no axe to grind. It also chimes somewhat with his personality as demonstrated by the notice he displayed in his porch.

- Mr Patterson says that the phrase "have some fun" is intended in an ironic sense. He referred in his evidence to his roots being in the north of the country, and to the sense of humour that prevails there. He gave an example that he says was comparable; if his car broke down, he might say "we will have some fun here", meaning the exact opposite.

- In my judgment, and for the reasons I have set out in the last but one paragraph, the expression "have some fun" demonstrates that Mr Patterson was indeed relishing the prospect of a visit by Newlyn. He was looking forward to a confrontation with them, during which he hoped and expected that he would triumph, and would demonstrate them and their staff to be foolish and inept, or worse. This would give him ammunition for his campaign against the council tax and its collectors.

- I am supported in this conclusion by a video film that was shown to me. It was posted on line. It is in effect a documentary centred on the events of 12th April 2018. It features a number of clips of an interview or interviews with Mr Patterson. And it shows video from 12th April 2018. Mr Patterson clearly, as he accepted, cooperated in its making. The respondents suggest it shows a lack of integrity on the part of Mr Patterson, and the video has been edited to give a knowingly false and misleading impression. I do not condemn the video in those terms. It is clearly designed to portray the events of that day from a particular point of view. The law respects, subject to limits, the right of individuals to publish their own views and their own "take" on events. Nobody with any normal degree of scepticism would regard that video documentary as a neutral or unbiased product. But Mr Patterson's participation in it does demonstrate a wish by him to continue his campaign against the council tax and those which seek to enforce his obligation to pay it.

Social media posts – Mr Binding

- Mr Binding was asked about posts that he had made on social media. He had used the words "arsewipe" and "tosser" to describe Mr Patterson. Those posts are at pages 80 and 81 of Mr Patterson's bundle of exhibits. I am unable to ascertain the date of those posts, but they appear (from the text of the posts) to be some nine months after April 2018. That would have been some months after Mr Binding has ceased to act as a CEA and surrendered his certificate. He explained that at the time he made those posts he was under considerable stress as a result of the complaint and the more general actions (including on social media) of Mr Patterson. Such posts are not edifying and do not reflect well on Mr Binding. But given the circumstances, and in particular that he had ceased to act as a CEA (and so could properly regard himself as less constrained than someone still holding such position), I do not regard that post as indicating that he is not a fit and proper person to hold the post.

Mr Wackett

- None of the actions of Mr Wackett suggest he is not a fit and proper person. He entered and remained on the property lawfully. The actions of Mr Binding did not require intervention by him. On the contrary, the situation in the house was heated. I think that there was a real risk, had he sought to become involved, that he would have inflamed matters. He had this in mind and referred, in his evidence, to the confined nature of the kitchen and the presence of knives in a kitchen. He remained calm but properly supportive of his colleague. To the extent that it is suggested that his attitude or actions were affected by his friendship with Mr Binding, I reject that. As with Mr Binding, I make no criticism of him for his choosing to leave from the area outside the property, or of the manner of his leaving.

Disposal

- In the circumstances, and for the reasons given, I dismiss the complaints against Mr Binding and Mr Wackett.

Costs

- The respondents apply for costs. The power to award costs is contained in, and only in, CPR 84.20(5) which provides as follows:

5) The court may order the complainant to pay such costs as it considers reasonable if it is satisfied that the complaint—

(a) discloses no reasonable grounds for considering that the certificated person is not a fit person to hold a certificate; and

(b) amounts to an abuse of the court's process.

Note that costs can be awarded only if both limbs of this test are satisfied.

- CPR 84.20(5)(a) requires the Court to be satisfied that the *complaint* (emphasis added) discloses no reasonable grounds. Sub-rules (2) and (3) make it clear (to the extent that this is necessary) that in the context of this rule, the "complaint" means the written document by which the complaint is made or initiated. It does not refer, in any wider sense, to the allegations made or case advanced by the complainant. That is consistent with the fact that there is no obligation on the complaint to attend any hearing or advance or prove his or her complaint.

- The wording in CPR 84.20(5)(a) has parallels with CPR 3.4(2)(a) which allows for the strike out of a statement of case which discloses no reasonable grounds for bringing or defending the claim. As CPR PD3A and the notes in the White Book (Civil Procedure 2019, para 3.4.2) indicate, this requires the Court to consider, and consider only, what is disclosed on the face of the statement of case. It does not permit an examination, still less an assessment, of the strengths and weaknesses of the evidence.

- Rule 84.20(5)(a) does not, in my judgment, allow the Court to analyse the strengths and weaknesses of the complaint when considering costs. The question is simply whether the written complaint discloses no reasonable grounds for considering that the certificated person is not a fit and proper person. That requires the assertions therein to be taken at face value. If it had been intended that the power to award costs (which is clearly the exception to the general position) would apply, for example, where the complainant has acted unreasonably or vexatiously in bringing or pursuing his complaint, it would have said so.

- Accordingly, I have no power to award costs.

Postscript to, and forming part of, judgment

- This judgment was circulated in draft to the parties, inviting them to submit a list of any typographical or other errors. The following (taking them in date order) were lodged at Court and forwarded to me;

    - First, on behalf of the Respondents, an email, pointing out (as well as a minor typographical error) that the draft judgment cited a superseded version of Reg 45 of the CT Regulations. I have taken account of that, and revised the draft judgment.

    - Second, a detailed critique of the judgment from Mr Patterson.

        - I have reviewed the draft judgment carefully in the light of that critique, but have made no consequent alterations to the above.

        - Mr Patterson's critique states that "I had no access to legal advice, only my McKenzie friend, Mr Docherty who was told could not speak to me, only hand me notes." I cannot recall whether I gave a formal instruction to the effect that Mr Docherty could not speak to Mr Patterson; I rather think it was more in the nature of a suggestion or request. In any event it was in response to the fact that on several occasions as Mr Patterson was addressing the Court, or as I was addressing him, Mr Docherty was pulling at his sleeve or top, causing Mr Patterson to break off to speak to him. Loud whispering between Mr Patterson and Mr Docherty was also occurring as Mr Royle addressed the Court. I formed the view that this was distracting to Mr Patterson (and unhelpful to him) and was likely to become distracting to me, Mr Royle and others in Court if not managed. In the event, there continued to be a degree of whispering between Mr Patterson and Mr Docherty, but at a manageable level.

        - I do not consider it necessary to respond to Mr Patterson's assertions as to at what stage a judge ought to find out the identity of the advocates who are due to appear before him or her.

DATED: 12th March 2020

N24 General form of judgment or order (4.99) Hertford County Court, PO BOX 373, Hertford, SG13 9HT

On 11th June 2020 I filed with the High Court an application for a judicial review of HHJ Rochford's judgement.

ATTACHMENT OF EARNINGS ORDER

Many people seem to believe that for the council to gain an attachment of earnings order they have to apply to a court, this is untrue.

The council are allowed to make their own order under The Council Tax (Administration and Enforcement) Regulations 1992

Making of attachment of earnings order
37.—(1) Where a liability order has been made and the debtor against whom it was made is an individual, the authority which applied for the order may make an order under this regulation to secure the payment of any outstanding sum which is or forms part of the amount in respect of which the liability order was made.

https://www.legislation.gov.uk/uksi/1992/613/regulation/37/made

What most employers don't realise is that also under The Council Tax (Administration and Enforcement) Regulations 1992 they can with good reason refuse to deduct money from an employees wages. A good reason being that for an employer to deduct money from an employees wages would put that employee in to financial hardship.

Offences
56.—(1) A person shall be guilty of an offence if, following a request under paragraph (2)(b) of regulation 36, he is under a duty to supply information and—

(a)he fails without reasonable excuse to supply the information in accordance with that regulation,

https://www.legislation.gov.uk/uksi/1992/613/regulation/56/made

An attachment of earnings order does not apply to the self-employed.

AMOUNT CORNWALL COUNCIL WERE OVERCHARGED FOR SUMMONSES BY THE MINISTRY OF JUSTICE

PAUL PATTERSON made this Freedom of Information request to Cornwall Council 7th August 2020

Dear Cornwall Council,
The Ministry of Justice said court fees for council tax summons had been set too high since 2013-4 following an "administrative error".

Could you please supply me with the following information: -
1. How much were Cornwall Council overcharged for each of the following years?
2. Have Cornwall Council now received a full refund?

2013-14
2014-15
2015-16
2016-17
2017-18
2018-19

Yours faithfully,

PAUL PATTERSON

Cornwall Council

Reference Number: FOI 101005054618

Response provided under: Freedom of Information Act 2000

Request:
Please provide me with the following information under the Freedom of Information Act 2000.

The Ministry of Justice said court fees for council tax summons had been set too high since 2013-14 following an "administrative error".

Could you please supply me with the following information:-

- How much were Cornwall Council overcharged for each of the following years?

- Have Cornwall Council now received a full refund?

    2013-14
    2014-15
    2015-16
    2016-17
    2017-18

2018-19

Response:

1. £0.00
2. N/A

The council tax summons fees were reduced from £3.00 to £0.50p per summons with effect from the 25 July 2018.

The new fee was implemented with immediate effect, which prevented any overcharges occurring.

Information provided by: Customer & Business Operations (Revenues)

Dear Revenues and Assessment - Freedom of Information
You state that," The new fee was implemented with immediate effect, which prevented
any overcharges occurring."

I think that you will find this incorrect. The Ministry of Justice erred with their summons charges from 2013 and overcharged councils from 2013.

The Ministry of Justice said court fees for council tax summons had been set too high since 2013-4 following an "administrative error". Councils had overpaid by about £9m a year since then, it said, and were entitled to be compensated in full.

https://www.litigationfutures.com/news/ministry-of-justice-admits-to-widespread-court-fee-overcharging

https://www.bbc.co.uk/news/uk-politics-44713630

I look forward to receiving a correct reply to my request.
Yours sincerely,

PAUL PATTERSON

10th September 2020
Information Classification: CONTROLLED

Dear Mr Patterson

Thank you for your email.

If you wish to know which organisations were compensated following the reform of Court Fees, which came into force from the 25 July 2018 you will need to contact the Ministry of Justice.

Kind regards

Mrs Liza Johnson|Assessment, Billing and Collection Technical Officer
Konsel Kernow/Cornwall Council| Customer & Business Operations

https://www.whatdotheyknow.com/request/amount_cornwall_council_were_ove#incoming-1637147

A TEMPLATE LEGAL NOTICE CHALLENGING ROCHDALE BOROUGH COUNCILS SUMMONS COSTS

NAME

LEGAL NOTICE
10th September 2020

FAO

Greater Manchester Magistrates

Clerk to the Justices

Greater Manchester Legal Team

Dear Greater Manchester Court,

I have been invited via a Council summons received from Rochdale Borough Council inviting me to a 'telephone hearing' sitting at Tameside Magistrates Court on 25th September 2020.

I understand from the Council summons that neither court nor magistrates can deal with or consider and take into account any of the following matters;

- Unable to pay
- Have applied for council tax support.
- Appealed to the valuation office for a deduction in council tax band
- Have appealed against a decision made by the council to hold you liable.

The summons from the Council also states, that I should speak to the council first; and that already summons costs of £101.50 have already been charged; yet even if I paid the whole amount today the Council will still be granted a Liability Order to the council for £101.50.

Therefore, in consideration of the above I will be challenging the councils costs.

I also desput that I have received a council tax reminder for this financial year.

Today a Freedom of Information Request has been made to Rochdale council as follows:

1. Will you please send me copies of a detailed breakdown of staffing costs and calculation approved by the magistrates for council tax summonses for:

2013-2014

2014-2015

2015-2016

2016-2017

2017-2018

2019-2020

2020-2021

2. How many names were on the bulk complaint list laid to the court for summonses to be issued on 28th August 2020, summonsing attendance to a 'telephone hearings' on 25th September 2020

3. Please give the name of the clerk to the justices who's signature is printed on the sumonses.

I immediately require of the court to;

- **Ensure I am given a certified copy of the original complaint made to the clerk to the justices**

- **Disclose how many other complaints were made by Rochdale Borough Council to clerk of the justices on 28th August 2020**

- **Disclose Rochdale Borough Councils 'detailed' break down of costs, as adding unreasonable costs not 'incurred' to the claim is unlawful.**

- **Disclose the section of the regulation or act which states a council tax summons hearing can be a 'telephone hearing.'**

- **Confirm that I am removed from the council's *'bulk order'* so that the court can deal with my matter individually; as I shall be asking for an adjournment, until these important issues can be addressed.**

I also bring the following to the courts attention:

I claim the Council has breached High Court Case ruling of: CO/976/2014

Rev Paul Nicholson v Tottenham Magistrates, because adding unreasonable costs to

the claim was unlawful.

IN THE SUPREME COURT OF JUDICATURE

COURT OF APPEAL (CIVIL DIVISION)

ON APPEAL FROM The Queen's Bench Division

The Administrative Court

Mr Justice Leveson

CO/6498/2003

"I find it very surprising that the only document with a court stamp (under xiii) is not produced by the court, but is created automatically by the local authority's software, even though the local authority is a party to the proceedings. (The example before us adds, under the court stamp, the words "Justice of the Peace for the area aforesaid (or by order of the Court Clerk of the Court)". The intended significance of these words is not clear to me.) This document apparently is used only for the purpose of confirming to the bailiff that he has power to act. However, for that purpose the rules require no more than "the written authorisation of the authority" (Non-domestic Rating (Collection and Enforcement) (Local Lists) Regulations 1989 r.14(5)). It seems both unnecessary, and wrong in principle, for it to be presented as though it had been stamped by the court. Nothing turns on this point in the present case, and we have not heard any submissions about it, but it seems to me an aspect of the procedure which merits reconsideration." LORD JUSTICE WALLER.

This notice has been sent to the relevant authorities in consideration of the seriousness of this matter and its potential wider implications. Please find my section 13A application attached.

I look forward to hearing from you in due course.

Yours Faithfully,

Name

Acct Ref XXXXXX   **Summons XXXXXXX**

Printed in Great Britain
by Amazon